THÍS BOOK
BELONGS TO:

_____

_____

_____

Praise for
My Friend Fox

'Blazingly beautiful and devastating. I wept but felt less alone as a human. I want everyone to read this book.'

– **Favel Parrett, author of *Past the Shallows* and *There Was Still Love***

'*My Friend Fox* is a beautiful memoir about experiencing diverse mental health. Heidi Everett is generous and gentle in sharing her story in order to demand a better mental health system for all.'

– **Carly Findlay, author of *Say Hello* and editor of *Growing Up Disabled in Australia***

'With breathtakingly original prose, Heidi Everett gently guides the reader through the complexities of living with mental illness. Humorous, heartfelt and humane, *My Friend Fox* is a deeply moving and essential read.'

– **Fiona Murphy, author of *The Shape of Sound***

'A raw and harrowing glimpse into life lived on the precipice, *My Friend Fox* boldly rips the facade from our sanitised perception of mental health treatment. And yet it is also tender and beautiful, with wisps of fable sprouting through the cracks; radiant art hewn from the darkness of the abyss.'

– **Bram Presser, author of *The Book of Dirt***

'If ever there was an authentic voice for survival from mental distress, then this is it. As painful as Heidi Everett's story is, it is told in the most inventive and magical way. Her use of language and imagery is that of a poet who constantly surprises and startles. Creativity and imagination are the soul food that nourish Heidi back to sanity. As does her dog, Tigger, her inseparable companion with whom she shares her life and struggles. This is a most wonderful book from a most wonderful writer.'

– Sandy Jeffs, author of *Flying with Paper Wings*

'This book is a story of reclamation, resilience and resistance. Heidi reclaims her story from the mental health industry that has defined her based on diagnoses and rewrites it as her own, rich, important experience which holds lessons for us all. *My Friend Fox* is an evocative and emotive memoir from an outstandingly talented writer. A must read for anyone who has ever felt on the outer.'

– Jax Jacki Brown, disability activist and writer

MY FRIEND FOX

HEIDI EVERETT

ultimo
press

Published in 2021 by Ultimo Press,
an imprint of Hardie Grant Publishing

Ultimo Press
Gadigal Country
7, 45 Jones Street
Ultimo, NSW 2007
ultimopress.com.au

Ultimo Press (London)
5th & 6th Floors
52–54 Southwark Street
London SE1 1UN

 A catalogue record for this
book is available from the
NATIONAL LIBRARY OF AUSTRALIA
National Library of Australia

My Friend Fox
ISBN 978 1 76115 015 9 (paperback)

Cover design Alissa Dinallo
Cover illustration Heidi Everett
Text design Simon Paterson, Bookhouse
Typesetting Bookhouse, Sydney | 11.6/17.7 pt Berkeley Oldstyle Pro
Copyeditor Ali Lavau

10 9 8 7 6 5 4 3 2 1

Printed in Australia by Griffin Press, part of Ovato,
an Accredited ISO AS/NZS 14001 Environmental Management System printer.

The paper this book is printed on is certified against the
Forest Stewardship Council® Standards. Griffin Press holds
FSC® chain of custody certification SGS-COC-005088. FSC®
promotes environmentally responsible, socially beneficial
and economically viable management of the world's forests.

Ultimo Press acknowledges the Traditional Owners of the country on which we work,
the Gadigal people of the Eora nation and the Wurundjeri people of the Kulin nation,
and recognises their continuing connection to the land, waters and culture.
We pay our respects to their Elders past and present.

I have no need of you. And you, on your part, have no need of me. To you, I am nothing more than a fox like a hundred thousand other foxes. But if you tame me, then we shall need each other. To me, you will be unique in all the world. To you, I shall be unique in all the world . . .

ANTOINE DE SAINT-EXUPÉRY,
THE LITTLE PRINCE

Dear Reader,

This letter is for anyone who comes to *My Friend Fox* with a story like mine. There are difficult things in these pages that I know many of us share.

I recommend that you only read on if you have the support of a good counsellor, or are at a point in life where you are able to hold others' stories safely.

Complex post trauma stress (PTS) is a lifelong reality and it can take many years of trial and error to learn how to live at peace with it; to know it's not your fault. It is not a disorder. It is an ongoing story of survival. To all my peers with living experience of diverse mental health, and to those yet to discover they are survivors, I offer my deepest respect.

Psych wards have the responsibility and the privilege to help people with PTS, to provide the tools of healing. Yet those of us who have spent time in these wards agree that healing is a long way off.

I hope *My Friend Fox* resonates in the psyche of a mental health system in equal need of healing.

Heidi

Lifeline 13 11 14

CONTENTS

ONLY THE MUDDY FOX LIVES

PHOKOJE GO TSELA O DITHETSENYA! they say in Botswana. *Only the muddy fox lives!*

The fox in this story isn't a scientifically-engineered, tame silver fox, but a wild, unwanted red fox. He's a descendant of a family who had no welcome, apart from the unknown bounty placed on their heads once arrived in a strange earth. He knows the crimson air is different to the red in his blood; it tastes drier, bigger, wider than his mother passed on to him. He notates the earth with dancing footprints yet the choreography is in a different key. At night, the stars are upside down and the heat, the heat, when the rain is more like snow—but there is no snow. Where is the snow? It must be hiding in the trees. The trees that smell like hedgehogs but sway like horses' tails on long summer evenings.

1

Fox does not belong; nor does he long to. A solved fox is a disappointment to his creed. He respects that everything around him is a stitch in a tapestry that took many moons to weave and that the moon was in another sky when his soul was being spun. He is fully alive, yet here he is, scrounging around in this field of the universe for five more minutes of heartbeat, 200 more breaths, another cognitive thought process, just like his cousins in the other earth. But Fox knows he is digging in a dirt that his ancestors never wore. He feels the weight of their old eyes, watching and waiting for him to give the clothes back. Put the clothes back, Fox. If he gives the clothes back, what will he wear?

Wherever Fox goes, he faces the dilemma. People despise him for his ways, yet his ways are as deep in spirit and creation as those of the people who shun him. He's a difficult one. Both predator and prey; a clever hunter who is forever hunted. His compass is true, but his tracks zigzag to confuse. He sits on the outer, waiting for me to discover him, because at the moment, I am on the outer too. He watches me. Can you see him? He's clever at hiding.

'Can they see us? Maybe they deliberately opt to keep
company with these strange birds in the psych ward cage.'

PÌGEONS ON A
BALCONY

THE COLD STEEL NEEDLE GOES into my right bum cheek
and the yellow oil is pushed in. Metal and veins never
mix well. Three nurses hold me down on the bed, my
face buried in the mattress. I scream, but the sound is
defeated by the noise in the back of my head. I struggle
to breathe, but there is no oxygen to be found in the
tiny space between my mouth and the plastic sheeting.

I'm angry as hell. The marauding invaders have
succeeded in their conquest and a great glob of heavy-
duty anti-psychotic is pulsating in my butt, radiating
into the rest of my flimsy human anatomy with the
unrelenting shock waves of an atom bomb. It's fractals
now: a picture Escher would be proud of. I survive
the hour-long seconds until I feel the pressure of a

thousand hands swiftly release me. My body springs back up from the bed. No longer part of a mattress, I fill my lungs with brittle, vile air.

I spin over and spit a vomit of abuse at the retreating posse. With their bulging backs they are as ugly as toads as they file out of my room. My deactivated body won't allow me to punctuate the room with a rainbow of action. They're now oblivious to my words anyway, a complete reversal of ten minutes ago, when I was scratching at the walls like a crazed cat in a stranger's hands. My head hurt. My heart hurt. My soul hurt. And now my body hurts.

Within this chemical straitjacket I am the final tiny babushka. It's keeping me contained in my amygdala, in my head, in my body, in my bed, in my room, in the ward, in the hospital. I'm sure I'm not the only one here who's dizzy from being confined to a 12 × 12-metre square common room for weeks, sometimes months on end. I've been here for six weeks and I still can't make out the horizon.

Confinement like this does funny things to an animal; it doesn't matter if it's for the benefit of the hostage. I once saw a Tasmanian devil lose his mind from captivity. The fearsome nugget of damned spite

*'Their bulging backs as ugly as toads
as they file out of my room.'*

had dissolved into the thousand-yard stare of an old teddy bear. He swayed on his two back feet, dancing a soft shoe shuffle to a swing band only he could hear. I yearned, craved, to rescue him from his healthy sanctuary and release him back to his cancerous freedom.

Here in this zoo of rescued souls, I mentally survey the psych ward while my body hallucinates about freedom. My bedroom—or should I say my room with a bed?—is number nine of twenty-eight identical rooms along two perpendicular corridors of about 50 metres each.

I have one white sheet covering a blue plastic mattress that farts if you sit down too quickly. The single metal-framed bed is bolted to the hard floor, as is the side table and cupboard with three shelves. There are no handles on the cupboard, so sometimes it's open, sometimes it's shut. But you can't choose. It mainly depends on who went through it last. There's a small scribble of graffiti on the wall just under the bedframe that can only be seen when I lie on my right side. It says *Love wins. Keep going* with a love heart underneath. It must have been written some time ago, as the ink has faded. I wonder how many other people have lain on bed nine thinking about love winning. Did they keep going?

Nearly every room has a toilet, shower and basin. These are cleaned once a day by a hospital worker with a mop and bucket. She—why always a she?—uses the same mop to wipe over the toilet, basin, shower floor and tap handles in every room. I have learned to remove my toothbrush and toiletries before she arrives. The rooms that don't have a bathroom are for the people who can't be trusted with such luxuries.

Beyond my room is the common room, the space broken in the middle by two whitewashed brick columns. Channel 10 is blaring endlessly on a vintage TV spruiking car ads to a man sprawled across five green waiting room chairs, his body somehow able to flow over the armrests. Two grey plastic tables over near the windows are studded randomly with seven white plastic chairs.

The furniture in the ward is sometimes arranged in a rectangle, sometimes in a square. But never a circle. Sometimes I want to smash the wall of unopening windows high above the staff car park. I don't want to watch them shift their cars three times a day. Cars come in; boom gate goes up. Cars go out; boom gate goes down. On Sunday, some fancypants hospital staff play tennis on the hospital's court. From my sniper position overlooking them, I can see the Chinese doctor always wins, with much exuberant celebration by all. The silver Mercedes is always parked diagonally across two spaces. The boom gate stays up on Sundays. I wonder if they play tennis on this day just to enjoy free, unfettered parking.

Luckily, I'm a smoker. That's my liberty. The only non-square thing in the common room is a white clock with black hands, hanging patiently over the screeching TV. It's interesting because it's the only thing in here that has real meaning in its mundane repetition. Repetition is torture to a creative brain. Yet fulfilled expectation is fundamental to a safe society.

I know it's a killer to be a clock-watcher, so I only take quick glances. When the ticking hand nears another fifteen-minute mark, it's exciting times! I shuffle slowly down the corridor to my bed at the end of the hallway, taking considered steps so as not to hurry up and waste time. I open my starchy white pillowcase and reach to the back of the fluff for my pack of PJs and lighter. Sweet—still there. Routine joy.

'A white clock with black hands, hanging
patiently over the screeching TV.'

Opening the door to the enclosed smoker's balcony, the thick grey cloud hits me with the energy of a jet exhaust and envelops me in a matriarchal hug. Oh, bliss. I'm not a psych patient in here. I'm a smoker! A scumbag smoker, making smoke and spending money on smoking disease. None of anyone else's business here; it's just me and my ciggie. As I puff and draw, I hear people muttering 'bad for you' . . . 'need to quit' . . . 'costs so much'. A different kind of head talk permeates the psych drawl. Keep it up.

I won't lie; the air in here is thick smog as I paddle my way around to another plastic chair pockmarked with melted cigarette burns and wringed out ash. Click click goes my lighter. Lovely sound. Draw back. Mmmm. Long breath out. I look at my new/old surroundings and take it all in again. Narrow concrete balcony. Red paint faded to the black-grey of what feels like a thousand years of soot. Hazy glass window, with high brick walls on either side so as not to tease with a glimpse of freedom. The bare walls are covered with layers of penned graffiti about love, death and psych wards. Plastic chairs move scratchingly here, there, back over here again.

'The thick grey cloud hits me with the energy of a jet exhaust and envelops me in a matriarchal hug.'

Talk out on the smoker's balcony is lighter than in the ward. Tough-sounding guys chat up skinny girls. Old hags squawk out tyrannical poetry. Young things, first-timers and gentle hunched-over people look nervously at their smoke ends, constantly checking progress. Screamers and dramatics yell their malignant innocence. Sad people stare down to hell through empty eyes, unable to reach their souls. Manic people wear their insides as their outsides, swapping randomly their outsides for their insides. Always someone on rations botting smokes off everyone else, poking through old ground-out stubs for one extra throat-grating gasp.

Pigeons on the ledge outside the glass sit in their own poo. They waddle along the knife-edge to another tasty squat. I watch the stupid birds. They're free to fly away, to go sit on a beautiful branch in a tall tree overlooking a park, but they choose to sit here. Can they see us? Maybe they deliberately opt to keep company with these strange birds in the psych ward cage. Maybe they think we're pigeons too. Pacing a small ledge, sitting in great pools of foul smoke. Protected behind glass wire.

~

14

Right now, though, I'm far away from that volcanic paradise.

I am squashed into the micro orbit of my bed, stuffed full of flupenthixol oil. I wish I could reach into my pillow and pull out a cigarette now, but my hand has become lifeless at the distant end of a long lump of rolled clay. Gravity multiplies. My mind is getting foggy. My muscles have no value.

I hate this place, obviously. I hate the smell of human fear that coats my tongue like a film of medieval dust. Sometimes I taste blood, piss and pheromones, mixed with the constant smell of industrial gravy and disinfectant. I manage to roll like a walrus flat onto my back and turn my weakening gaze up to the collapsing ceiling. I let my sight flop around the steady landmarks of the heavenly square for comfort. Familiar Air Vent, oh how happy I am to see you there!

My eyes prickle with tears. Am I crying? What real use is there of brine filling up and overflowing the sidewalls of these eye sockets? Trickling, flowing wet salt drips into my ears. I admonish the sobbing. These tears are as useless as the cries of a family labrador in the jaws of a bogan's pit bull.

Ah, but there's Fire Detector on the ceiling over near the door. Through the stained glass of my rain-soaked vision, I see the sweet little round satellite hanging fearlessly from the indoor sky. It has a similar insurgent spirit to that of the clock: a shape that doesn't belong in this geometric cartoon and a ticking mind that would drive you mad if you weren't using it to keep you sane. I study the cute little black tester button set wonky in the casing. I wonder if the button has the character of an army major. 'Stand to attention! On the ready! Do you want me to make a test sound now? Now? Now? Now?' Stand down.

My eyes roll up and back, up and back through oculogyric crisis. My mind is dragged downwards into a heavy damned sleep. There I go, wings clipped and luggage discarded. I tumble around in the deep dark coma, senses flailing, trying to grasp something solid. I'm conscious enough to know that saliva is drooling from the corner of my mouth onto my clean pillow. I'm ashamed of the dirty puddle. I hope no one sees it. For a short time, I dream I have a nice clean pillow. The primitive need to urinate seeps into my awareness. There's no hope dreaming now, so I just imagine I'm on the toilet. Plastic sheets, at least.

I also imagine, maybe too believably, that I'm dying. It's a good feeling. My heart skips a beat and I look forward to seeing Jesus and all my angel family. I float higher and higher. The sky goes from pitch-darkness to brilliant lightness. Up, up I go. Is there no end to this wonder flight? I have no need for my despised mortal lump now in this place where gravity is upside down. Up here I somersault and dive. One push and I soar up past a star system; I travel thousands of light years with hardly any effort. I surmise that this dark matter is some kind of universal water. Fish can't see the water they swim in, so why should we carbon-based forms see the matter we live in? Until we're fished out, at least.

Suddenly I'm aware there are ropes. I feel a horrendous burning way back down in my body; my wings are bound too tightly to sinews that have stretched too far. My soul screams in pain. I can't work out why it hurts so much. Oh Lord, save me from this torture. I try to urge myself back into the cool, fresh, free space again, but the stretching is contracting and urgently pulling me back. The cosmic lightness is displaced by a violent darkness, shuddering away all traces of joy. Every cell in my body reclaims ownership of existence, and my consciousness plummets back to my body like a NASA capsule returning to Earth.

There is a jarring thump. My heart takes a massive leap and I'm shoved back into a senseless silence. I'm choking in a mass of thick fluid that is both inside and outside of me. The darkness gets darker, the coldness becomes ice. I stay down here, frozen, for a long time as the last of my spirit is extinguished. My fingers stretch out in search of physical contact but there is none. Trapped bones in my fingers yearn to become feathers but they are un-evolved batwings. I struggle to make myself aware of my struggle. I don't give up. I am a survivor. It's such a long-time struggle.

25,879 (OR PART THEREOF)

BANG BANG! WHAT'S THAT? BANG bang again! I feel air sweep into my lungs and my eyes flicker with light. Bang bang bang! What the hell? My brain reboots slower than a Commodore 64 but it's enough to realise where I am. The banging turns out to be Anonymous Nurse #36 whacking on the door to tell me its mealtime—aka meds time.

How long have I been out for? There's no way to tell. I climb out of my coffin and stumble out into the corridor. I'm suddenly very big, very heavy and very, very tired as I slouch along to the common room. I don't recognise myself in the reflection in the windows. Where's that girl with the hard-won higher school certificate gone? The girl who can freestyle twenty laps of the pool non-stop, the four-wheel-driving jillaroo who learned to negotiate inverted terrain while tutoring a petrified passenger on the mysterious nocturnal habits of the long-footed potoroo (*Potorous longipes*)? Where's my wry smile, clear skin, sun-bleached hair, my female form? All identifying features are trapped on a golden disc reaching the furthest limits of our sun and suffering termination shock.

As the light in me dims, I catch fraying embers of my drifting past. I look down at my idle hands and imagine how they hauled hay bales out to cows in dusty paddocks from the tray of a driverless ute, entrusted with first gear. It reminds me there's a knack to opening heavy bags of grain: cut the string right and the bag pops open like velcro; cut it wrong and the string becomes your enemy. The macramé tightens as you wrestle the worsening knots, your fingers unable to grasp any threads. You end up with a wretched sack full of tattered holes and grain all over the floor.

I study the tips of my fingers. They are the same ones I had before but they haven't touched my favourite things for so long. Slumped at a common room table, I slowly trace the outline of a horse on the white plastic to see if I can remember. The newly formed creature senses life and inhales in air and carbon. Its body breaks free from the table, rearing boldly, with a majestic head and flourishing tail providing the perfect cantilever.

The sudden animation startles me. Under my finger, the rearing equine is quietened down into an elegant piaffe: a feat of galloping and standing at the same time, in a perfect show of force and control, going everywhere but going nowhere. I decide to tame the beast altogether and, with a few soft strokes, it drops into an ambling walk, finally coming over and looking at me dopily, hoping for a carrot. With one more breath it is gone and the sunlit Viennese arena becomes a plastic hospital tabletop.

Here I am, in a public psych ward. In this place, I am not creation. I'm a plasticine blob being shaped by a medical sculptor into a humanoid form. I am no longer girl.

I am psych patient number 25,879* (or part thereof). *Age: 24. Primary diagnosis: schizoaffective. Comorbidity: major depression, ? juvenile autism. Seems to enjoy music, art. No dependents.* No further use for a name.

I stand in line at the meal trolley. It's an ugly contraption to match the ugly ward. Beige plastic trays of hot cooked dinners in neatly stacked rows of four. Each tray is endowed with a plastic knife, fork and spoon. I'm so hungry I can't wait to sit down and gorge on my delicious fare of boiled potato, soggy slivers of beef, beans and rotting gravy. Dessert is vanilla ice cream and tinned fruit. In it goes, down it slides, no need to chew. It's all so soft and comfortable. The meal is gone in three minutes. I scour the food trolley for untouched trays. There are a few, so I take one and throw the contents down my gullet. Why, I should squawk like a seagull!

I have no idea that the meds are causing insurmountable hunger. No one here does, perhaps not even the staff. We snout around the meal trolley like pigs. Some really big men take pickings off discarded plates, greedily licking their fingers of the last vestige of the salty gravy. I see that there is a microsecond delay before they realise they can't eat their fingers too.

We line up for chasers. Another trolley has been surreptitiously wheeled out behind us while we were distracted by the food. This time, instead of swarming the opportunity, we line up before the altar at which a nurse bestows on each of us two little clear plastic cups.

I notice the behaviour of people in front of me as they receive the Eucharist. Some grumble and growl and take a long time to negotiate back to nothing except

'I can't wait to sit down and gorge on my delicious fare of boiled potato, soggy slivers of beef, beans and rotting gravy.'

'Another trolley has been surreptitiously wheeled out
behind us while we were distracted by the food.'

the pills. Thin, grey mystics accept the pills with bowed heads and move on to the next stage of enlightenment with formidable grace. Others seize the chance to practise stand-up comedy and ask the nurse why she's not dispensing cash, lollies or drugs. She is.

It's my turn. I humbly step up to the high priestess and internally bless myself. She's a good two feet shorter than me but she seems ten feet taller. How can she be looking up at me and down at me at the same time? It's a trick of the eye performed by all psych ward staff. She flicks through a big folder and must find the symbol that reveals my identity. She makes a tick next to it with her pen-on-a-string and from an array of blister packs pops two pills—one big and white, one small and pink. Plop they go into a cup, which she hands to me with an accompanying little chalice of water, barely enough to wet a raindrop. Compared to many in here, my cup of pills is Medication Lite. I quickly wonder if anyone else sees; my street cred will drop even further.

None of us have any idea how much these chemicals are really affecting us, so we just take the damn things. We have no choice anyway. If we resist anything in this place, we end up back on our mattress with another needle stabbed into our butt. If we make a big old fuss, we are dragged into solitary, to stare insanely at our own hallucinations on the generous canvas of blankness.

There's a nondescript door near the nurse's station that people are ushered through when they yell too much. Men with blue gloves arrive, circling the prey as any skilled team of predators would. The yelling person, playing the part of herd animal, continues their theatre, maybe kicking their heels up to show peak fitness, or swerving this way and that to demonstrate agile dexterity. The predators quietly, calmly move closer, closing off escape routes. As in all realistic nature documentaries, the weakening gazelle is pounced upon when it lunges left instead of right. The blue-gloved lions transport their screeching, desperate meat away, through the door, never to be seen again. Another similar-looking person emerges six or twelve days later, fresh as a daisy and ready to rejoin the herd.

~

There are many unwritten rules in any institution. These are far more consequential than the operational rules inflicted by boring old protocol. There are no guidelines on the wall about etiquette around other patients or how to navigate the empty routine of the day.

No nurse reads out your rights or tells you breakfast is at eight, lunch is at twelve, dinner is at five. No doctor says you will leave the ward when you tolerate the medication agreeably and stop trying to kill yourself. You just absorb these things through osmosis.

These unspoken rules are written in trees, in broken TV remote controls, in puffs of cigarette smoke and the sound of flip-flops slapping up and down the hallway all day long. Rules are bound up in the stitches of people's odd socks and the mountain of polystyrene cups discarded along with spilled Milo tins. They float in on the scent of a visitor's perfume and leave with the magpie who flew over to peck at a tiny spider under a grey stone outside your bedroom window. These rules bend and sway and ebb and flow with the breathing of time and the flexing and fluxing of space. They are bright flashes of luminance caught in the eye and they are shadows of movement tasted not seen.

Through this slow-burn realisation I work out that people leave the place when they smile, laugh, participate enthusiastically in art therapy, speak the words of psychiatrian to the psychiatrists. These people wear clothes of confident socialisation with their domestication. As one of the majority who wants to get out of this place, I decide I will need to do the same.

At first, I just observe. So much is learned through observation. The psych staff know this; their whole careers are based on practising observation. As a player, even if just the pawn, it pays to know a little of the history of psych wards. In the early days of asylums, patients were diagnosed by popular vote. If someone was behaving like they were distracted by invisible forces, they were labelled 'psychotic'. This included those who were deaf, autistic, spasmodic, overworked mothers, men with head wounds and even wives and daughters whose husbands and fathers surmised they were psychotic, even though the husbands and fathers were the only ones to be distracted by it. Local people were trained as asylum nurses on the job by the hospital physician, and most often these people were just bricklayers and blacksmiths looking for paid work.

In the spirit of the game, I carry on observing. I see the most popular nursing staff and psychiatrists stay out on the savanna to hang around one or two particular patients. These people seem to have a bit of street-tough attitude compared to the mystics and me. I deduce that cheekiness must appeal to those from private school backgrounds, unused to cheeky poverty and cheeky abuse. The patients deemed worthy of attention swear quite a bit, are loud in their demands, thought processes and social jostling, and constantly make quips about farts, arseholes and cunts. They're walking Instagram, Facebook and Twitter feeds, so everyone knows their current mood and what they're going to do about it. Like.

There's nothing about me that any of the staff seem to aspire to know. Most days come and go without me registering a single blip on the ward's seismograph. I can't help but feel unloved, but then I have to remind myself that this is a psych ward, not a Tinder account. The only times I've garnered attention were upon arrival, when my energy still hovered around nuclear fusion, and when my blood gets fizzy from too much sugar, carbs and caffeine and not enough activity to burn it. But even then, I am a mere gazelle. It's rare that anyone enters the psych ward as anything other than a gazelle—unless they are on drugs. Then they are the lion.

My only real expression of anarchy is getting up and walking out of art therapy each fortnight when the therapist gleefully starts guiding us in sticking psychedelic fake feathers onto paper plates with clag and saying, 'This is the real you.' Or music therapy, when a heavily guarded acoustic guitar is unshackled from its safe in the wall and the visiting music therapist hands out 1970s folk songs for us to sing along with while she dreams of being Joni Mitchell.

If I'm to get out of this place, I need to develop my larrikin appeal. Spending time in the country on horseback and growing up in one of the toughest suburbs in Australia, I know the traits. I begin strolling, lolling and drawling. Instead of giving off an aura of shyness, intellect and reserve, I work on my Aussie cockney, which I start to pepper into my daily dialogue of not-much.

A stout, ruddy woman in pyjama shorts and flip-flops whom I haven't yet had the opportunity to relate to personally approaches me in the hallway. 'How ya garn?' I say as she flip-flops past. She looks at me. I feel myself blush. Like I've just told her she's an idiot and I don't like her choice of footwear. 'Alright,' she offers without any inflection. As she walks past, her eyes stay on me. My mind races through the possible outcomes— a punch in the face, spit on my back, a nasty rumour spread about my thumbs, all my belongings gone.

Unlike in my school days, I take offensive action. I see her again that afternoon on the smoker's balcony with a group of similar linguists. I sit next to her, look out the window (not at my feet) and pull back hard on my ciggie, which I'm holding between my thumb and forefinger. 'Jeez, it's so fucking boring in this place,' I growl. I await the verdict. 'Yeah, I reckon,' her mate chucks back. Okay, we're in. Normally I'd say something about the pros and cons of exercise and the need to address the imbalance of unspent cortisol in sedentary people who are clinically psychotic, but on this occasion I say nothing, just nod and check the glowing end of my ciggie. The target reveals her soft belly and masters it all by saying, 'Be so fucking funny if we trashed the fucking place!' Everyone laughs and I started it. Win.

~

Over the course of a few days, I realise that my efforts are succeeding with other patients, but not with the staff. They still have no interest in me. I need to tweak my style. I decide I must crack the code of the hospital, not just the people snared in its roots. Thinking more like a spy, I start to gather intelligence by participating in collaborative reconnaissance missions with other patients. Using my new cockney charm, I persuade a few people on the cusp of being discharged to reveal the secrets to their success. 'Anything to fuck over the bastards!' is the attitude. 'Yeah, I reckon,' I reply. It's like learning a foreign language, but I know it's necessary.

My early attempts at subterfuge don't work. The doctor is more interested in the .doc version of me in my file than the organic person sitting in front of him. I perform my routine over and over, each time tweaking a little more, seeing where the doctor flinches and where he folds. I listen to where his timbre shifts from coniferous to angiosperm (needle-like to fruit-bearing). Going into the office each Tuesday and Friday is another round of Shakespeare, but with the perseverance of mankind, I eventually make it to the next level: a big room full of doctors.

I go into the big room on a Monday, Wednesday and again the following Monday. I sit at one point of a giant triangular table looking up at three colossal doctors and three titanic nurses. I still don't know how they make everything so big on their side and so tiny on mine. The well-dressed people rock back in their chairs, chew pens, flick pages, punch numbers

'I sit at one point of a giant triangular table looking up
at three colossal doctors and three titanic nurses.'

into calculators and check the vital signs of well-fed clipboards. It makes me think I'm in the wrong room and this is, in fact, a meeting of company accountants going over the monthly budget.

The result of the first seminar with the accountants is nothing. In the second, I'm granted two hours of day release. This means being escorted in the psychiatric van to a nearby park. The white eight-seater bus has seatbelts and vertical bars on the windows. We patients climb in the back with stiffened muscles not used for weeks. Everyone immediately asks to get out to have a smoke. We all clamber out again then, five minutes later, get back in. The belts go on and the windows inch open through the bars. The psych nurse is a cheery man with a German accent. He ensures no one needs to go to the toilet, but the mention of it puts the thought in everyone's head, so the sliding door opens again and people get out. Ten minutes later, we're all back in the bus, the door slams shut and the cheery man at the wheel proclaims we're off to the park. Halfway there, a ginger-bearded man in the back seat shouts that he needs to vomit so the van pulls over to the side of the road and the poor man vomits out the door. We spend half an hour being dragged around the nearby park before everyone sprints back to the bus, overwhelmed with the claustrophobia of empty space.

My promotion to day release is secured by my verbal observation at my next bookkeeper hearing. I remark that the woman doctor is looking more stressed than me—a perfectly executed witticism that earns me applause and a secret handshake. But I only make it as far as the staff car park before disassociating. To fill the sudden vacuum of restraint, I walk up and down the rows of cars studying number plates, which also satisfies my desire for useful information. However, I pass the psych ward freedom test by flying back to the coop without blowing anything up, and the next Monday I'm again granted full day release. I walk down to Coles to buy a carton of cigarettes and I stop at McDonald's on the way back. It all looks and sounds like freedom, but my cheeseburger stinks of hospital gravy and my strawberry thickshake grates on my teeth like a polystyrene coffee cup.

One more weekend of brain-numbing boredom, and the following Monday morning the accountants tell me I can stay out overnight if someone is with me. No one is with me, so I spend the day filling giant plastic bags with second-hand clothes in Savers before coming back to my bed in the ward. This third dutiful return means I pass the final audition, and at the end of eight weeks of creative development and dry rehearsals, I play the role of 'recovered patient' to critical acclaim, take my curtain call and walk offstage. Bravo!

Here's the script for you, should you ever find yourself in this situation:

My symptoms do dissipate when I take the much-higher dose of this antipsychotic.

I realise I do need help to regain control over the voices and delusions. Thank you so much for making that clear to me.

I agree to be placed on this community treatment order and see my doctor and case worker regularly. And even if those people should change every six weeks, I am happy to retell my entire family history over and over, answering the same six questions, and I shall do it with enthusiasm and gratitude every time.

Yes, ongoing acute clinical depression sometimes does need a course of ECT to help the brain recalibrate the chemical dopamine and serotonin imbalance, depleted through no fault of mine. In

'My Certificate of Achievement freshly stamped and signed.'

just the same way diabetics need insulin to maintain a healthy lifestyle, so too do I need a lifetime of synthetic to biological infusion to relieve any stress factors that may influence my genetic disposition towards aggravated mental ill-health in the future.

(Tip: It's really important to practise eye contact on other patients first, if eye contact isn't easy for you. The doctor has laser eyes.)

~

One anonymous sunny day, I take my first steps out through the constantly beeping and clicking doors with my Certificate of Achievement freshly stamped and signed, into the world I left two months earlier. It doesn't matter that I'm going home to six months' worth of psychotic suicidal cobwebs, uncollected garbage, unwashed bedsheets stiff with sweat and maggots in the sink—I'm going home.

The question 'Who am I now?' is everywhere I walk. Fox has grown up and left home too and has noticed my unsteady footprints in the dirt.

SETT

It took quite a few cycles around the sun for the dropped seed of a chinwag with some angels in my bedroom at four years old to germinate and ripen into being admitted to the psych ward and diagnosed schizoaffective at twenty-four. That kind of tree takes many seasons to grow, but it could've been tended into quite a different plant altogether in the lands of another farmer. I was relatively lucky. I grew up in the remote Welsh–English borderlands with quiet, earthy parents who did the best they could with the bits and pieces they found discarded by the side of the road. They didn't have much money, but between Dad's modest wage as a skilled toolmaker and Mum's ability to make a hot meal out of a bag of crisps, my parents were able to provide us kids with morals, ethics, safe and clean housing, and the best birthdays and most magical Christmases you could imagine. It didn't take much to make a magnificent Christmas when snow was falling and Father Christmas knew a child loved horses and sweets.

Socially, however, our family was an island on an island surrounded by moats of jagged rocks and raised drawbridges. Maybe it's because paranoia toils deep in our blood. I'm guessing paranoia would've come in handy various times through eons of war, disease, invasions, civil unrest, pagan rituals and religious chess. Generation upon generation of my ancestors evolved me a great set of antisocial traits to ensure the best chance of survival against other people. My family blood is so thick with suspicion, we can't hug each other in case one of us is carrying a weapon (we're not), nor show a skerrick of mortal weakness in case we're branded common.

As it turns out, my in-built knack for film noir meant I lived through my younger years relatively unscathed, but the punchlines from dark jokes resonated long after. Traps that were loaded and set in my childhood went off with the slightest nudge in my adulthood because the psychological hunters knew their quarry was a long-term project and were prepared to wait.

Like many young girls, all I wanted was a horse. But no amount of wishing brought me a fairy godmother to bring me that horse, so drawing them made me all the horses I could dream of. Anywhere there was blank space, I drew me up a horse—on the inside covers of library books, on the margins of Dad's newspaper, on discarded toilet rolls, in remnants of chocolate pudding scraped around the bowl with a spoon, on fogged-up windows, a crumpled blanket pulled up to my chin. I saw invisible horses everywhere and loved bringing them into my world. Mum took me to a pony-riding school a few times, but the shock of being around real horses and the seemingly random movement of four feet under my already discombobulated two, combined with English mud slurry everywhere the horse stepped, overwhelmed my brain into utter terror. I screamed in panic when the girl leading my pony asked it to step over a tiny log. I went back to drawing.

Apart from my horse drawings and a bunch of schoolkids singing about being stuck in brick walls, there wasn't much notable art being produced in our 1970s backwater. I'm guessing that, as Leonardo would've discovered in his time, art had to satisfy the working man and woman's idea of imagination. It had to

*'I screamed in panic when the girl leading my
pony asked it to step over a tiny log.'*

be utilitarian or it was pointless. To fulfil this proviso, I sketched horse's legs, heads and hooves in various poses until they were mechanically correct and fit for the user in whatever situation they might find themselves. I wanted to look at my horse and consider it beautiful but I wanted my parents to look at my horse and agree it was operational.

My other favourite thing was being outdoors. It's harder to re-create the illusion of nature on paper, so with my horses trapped controllably in two dimensions, space and time was painted alive by just by stepping out my front door. Fields of wheat, sheep and dairy cows played tick-tack-toe up the rise to our garden, fringed by persistent brooks and medieval hedgerows with tangled briars tumbling out like spring clouds. It was easy for me to be out there in nature. Our 300-year-old stone cottage sat at the last stitch on the hem of a tiny village on a sliver of road between two country towns. The only passers-by were local farmers and townspeople who'd taken the wrong road home on a day out in the neighbouring country, just twenty miles away. In this part of the world, going over the council boundary took six months of planning and reconnaissance trips

'I sketched horse's legs, heads and hooves in various poses.'

to the post office, supermarket and confession. Our front door opened me up to it all.

Like many countrified people, my parents harboured a deep mistrust of other people, so we never had visitors and we never visited anyone. I grew up with no teaching or understanding of other humans other than my tormenting brother and the fearsome Old Man Down the Road and Witch who Lived in the Hedge (in reality, a middle-aged widower and a Gypsy). Apart from school, and an expedition to see my grandparents in December, my entire social development was shaped by my inherited imagination, the animals, plants, the seasons and the occasional UFO that coloured it in. Civilisation to me was a seething ocean of aliens, the Devil and God, depending on what mood the day was in. Science, medicine and sinister neighbours only completed a collusion of trickery. This upbringing was no fault or gift of my parents, but just like any diverse ideology, our tribe tasted the earth a little differently from that of the meat-and-three-vegetables kind. We were a bowl of bananas.

Education, not surprisingly in our motionless village, carried forth the monocles and switches of old school headmasters and spiky blackboard mistresses. I hated it and, with equal passion, that English primary school hated me. I was a messy, untameable child with no budding potential in learning the art of people, so the teachers' way of accommodating me was to ignore me altogether. At the age of eight, I was sat with my knees hard against the side cupboard of the St Weonards class-room while all the other pupils sat at neat little tables of four, sharing coloured pencils, swapping Shrinky Dinks and inventing Roald Dahl-esque nicknames for the infamous pariah, Heidi the Snotty Nose.

By year three, I should've been able to fumble some kind of crude human alliance, but without any workable skills in that little corker *theory of mind*, all I did was observe, through a deep majestic river of snot dangling from my nose and soggy pickled underwear clinging to a raw, itchy bottom. From the moment I trudged into the school hall in the morning to the moment I closed my eyes at night, my psyche was littered with a daily ritual of teasing, degradation and humiliation, and all without any understanding that it wasn't supposed to be like this.

Everyone was different from me but I didn't know how.

THE COW

I TAKE A FEW MOUTHFULS of grass, allowing my mercurial silver tongue to curl around the fresh stems and pull. How do I describe what grass tastes like? It's salty. My body craves salt. It might have something to do with the fact that both grass and I evolved from the sea. Every five mouthfuls, I look up a bit and chew the jumble in my mouth into a fat sausage shape to swallow down into my body. It's a nice habit.

The day is coming from the west, so I push my eyes and ears to the creek occasionally. I like to see what's around me all the time because prevention is better than cure. There are things that live and move under the scramble of tea-trees but they don't really bother me. Not like the humans who come down from the farmhouse riding horrible little ponies.

Horses and cows do not get along. Horses are bossy because they know humans idolise them. They bully me just because they want to eat the same stalk of grass I'm aiming for—not because they have to, but because they can.

I know the fox is there. It thinks I don't realise but of course I do. It's just that, as a cow, I'm blasé. I don't hyperventilate like other field creatures do when there's the tiniest hint of a threat. Right now, the fox is on tippy-toes, trying to get from one side of the paddock to the other without me noticing. I always notice, and when I do I flick my right ear to say, 'Seen you.' I've learned the game because I've played it fifty million times already. The first few times I thought it was a dog.

Dogs are a different story. They're much worse than horses because dogs see me as food. As far as I know, I'll live out my days in this paddock, offering my udders and motherly shelter to poddy calves who've outlived their own mothers. A dog in my field will be chased down and stamped on by me. That's a rule.

Foxes, on the other hoof, don't share the pack-hunting mentality of dogs. They are soloists in the orchestra of hierarchy. The only fox that could try to take me down is the gigantic one that Zeus turned

'I know the fox is there.'

to stone and flung up into the night sky. Apparently, that fox was so big and powerful that it couldn't be killed—until someone found a magical dog that was able to catch and destroy anything. Unfortunately, the bureaucrats didn't realise the two had opposing abilities: one was able to keep moving and the other was able to stop anything. They cancelled each other out. In the end, Zeus chucked them both into the sky and solved the problem for all.

The little fox is now running past my feet as I'm speaking; the bloody thing did get past without me realising. I'm no good at multitasking. Talking to you about an ancient Greek story, chewing grass into a sausage and reacting to a puny fox simultaneously is not in my skill set. So if you don't mind, this conversation is over.

ANOTHER TOWN, ANOTHER SHOW

AFTER MY FIRST RELEASE FROM the acute adult psychiatric unit, I make the trip home on the bus with fresh air in my lungs and a reset perspective on the world around me. Everything seems to be operating with a newly painted coat of normality. The trees are trees, cars move around like cars and road signs point to roads. While the bus lumbers along, I recalibrate society by noticing people going about their business. It's perplexing that all these people continued doing all these normal things while I was away being totally abnormal. Through the window, I see they still park their cars in the IGA supermarket car park and are going in to buy their groceries. Hungry Jack's up on the corner is still taking orders from people in the drive-through and the servo has people putting petrol in cars at the pumps.

The road is still potholed and the roadside grass leans over gravel kerbs with the dual weight of neglect and prosperity. I get out one street away from home and, although the sun's out, a breeze snakes in from the lowlands and it steals the warmth of town. My bags are heavy. I managed to buy half of Savers and it seems like the few items I had brought to the hospital from home have bred multiple generations.

As I enter my unit, the stink of stagnant fear welcomes me in with gnarled fingers and a tortured nose. I open all the windows and step out the back door to be greeted by a tall grass forest. Last time I was out here, I lay on the lawn for hours, unable to move due to a complete loss of cognitive wherewithal. I decide to have a shower to clear my thoughts and repot the dead air. Unlike the gentle shower in the psych ward, the water splurts out of the old showerhead, hitting my skin like rusty meteors and gunfire cracks in my ears. I wash off the soap as fast as I can, wincing with sensory overload but determined to face this homecoming with a freshly laundered body.

Like on the ward, there's nothing to do but at least now I'm free to do it. I buy and eat copious bags of Coles brand cheese rings to fill the abyss of time and space, and I like them so much I have them for breakfast, lunch and tea. I drink lots of beer. I go through a cheap slab every two days while smoking lots of cigarettes. I watch TV and listen to cassette tapes. The meds make me sleep too much and, for some reason, night-time becomes daytime. Someone once told me that it's known as schizophrenia-time.

My day starts at 9 pm and ends at 7 am. My only occupations are purchasing more cheese rings and beer and moving my things around my flat like a giant game of one-sided chess. I don't see anyone apart from a ferret of a neighbour who walks past my window every night and morning on his way to and from work. He's a Jehovah's Witness and has gleefully informed me I will be his wife when we meet in heaven, along with Kylie Minogue and five other women I don't know. I haven't told him I don't go for small men who smell like mothballs and have giant Elvis sideburns.

Strange things haven't stopped completely; I lied when I told the doctor my symptoms had dissipated. I dream twenty-four hours a day and I'm never sure

'I buy and eat copious bags of Coles brand cheese rings to fill the abyss of time and space.'

what's real and what's not so real. Ironically, the word 'schizophrenic' is written on doorhandles and promoted on the side of buses. I wonder if schizophrenia is a self-fulfilling prophecy. Alien–human hybrids knock on the door of my unit with their hypnotic evangelism and I swoon in terror in front of them. In a trance, I tip a glass of water onto a power socket for a reason my mind never tells me. There are cameras in the wall plaster. The police helicopter chases me into my flat. I change my Alanis Morissette tape to side B without moving.

Wearing dark baggy clothes that suit my intolerance for frequencies of any energy, I begin to meander around town through the dark, night-time still feels so much safer. This is my world: a world where I earned my breakdown over nearly a decade of antisocial pinball. In the muted half-light and semitones of society, I go into rough pubs and drink cheap tap beer with the old alcoholics because we silently speak the same language. That's all you need to fit in: the scent of decay. The men are the sort of blokes you'd find in rural Australia, but they don't bother much with a tall, weird woman sitting on a stool next to them. If they do ask, it's over in three seconds when I fling back one of the lines I mastered in the psych ward: 'Got a problem? Nah, din't think so. Finsh yer beer.'

A highly unconventional fight breaks out in my preferred bar between a manic musician high on coke and the most wasted German backpacker I've ever seen. To step away from the situation, I venture across the road to the small hotel called Nine Cats with a quiet youngish man who thinks the same. Over the years, the Nine Cats building has changed ownership a number of times. Until recently, it was a brothel. The building perches awkwardly on the south side of the four-pub intersection, and somehow looks like it was transported from Pudding Lane before the Great Fire. Its wanton leering through blacked-out windows exudes danger but I'm curious to see what a brothel layout might be and it helps that there's a big sign out the front that says 'Free Pool on Wednesdays'. The quiet youngish man and I agree we'll have a game.

I like playing pool. As with drawing horses, geometric design comes alive in my mind and I appreciate the satisfying click as two balls hit. It's even better when that mental architecture and click send a ball into a pocket with that cocooning *wooollibilloobily* sound. I've had quite a lot of practice at pool. In my teens, an equally disjointed friend and I hustled pool tables in nightclubs and pubs around south-eastern Melbourne under-suburbs. We weren't close friends. We just had an unspoken agreement to hang out together arising from a shared love of horses, a distrust of people and a penchant for playing pool with drunk men who thought we were the dorkiest women they'd ever seen in a nightclub, but the best type to lose to at pool. No shame in being beaten at pool by an ugly, dorky woman.

The entrance to Nine Cats is up a dark, steep, narrow staircase pinpricked by red lights. I wonder if the brothel is still operating and 'free pool' means something else entirely. My drinking companion is behind me on the steps so I can't turn around and go back without causing some kind of warp in the space–time continuum, so I keep going. I emerge into what seems an unlit room, but the soundtrack of pub voices encourages me to readjust my eyes. I finally make out a small bar etched into the corner and a posse of drunk businessmen, either former patrons still hanging on to the last vestige of hope or men without souls.

In the glow of a light with the strength of a candle, I make out the pool table over near a blacked-out window. Although my nerves are starting to get the

'The entrance to Nine Cats is up a
dark, steep, narrow staircase.'

better of me, I rack up the table with the satisfying routine I follow every time, finishing with the 'plonk' of the eight ball into its middle slot. I don't feel good, but my new friend breaks and I wonder aloud if we have to buy a drink. I don't want to, not in here. I'm acutely aware that the posse of men have now all turned, are looking our way, and that their voices have developed a tone I don't like. I don't want to go to the bar; I don't want to go near them.

A big part of me wishes the game were over so we could leave. It's my turn, so I fix my shot on the orange ball in the top left pocket. An awkward shot, but my favourite. With my wonky eyesight I have a bias for crookedness and rarely do I pot a straight shot. As I take the hit, a voice calls out from the posse, 'Hey, have you got a driver's licence?'

I look up. 'Me?'

'Yeah, we want to see your age,' the unidentifiable voice replies.

There's a sibilant 's' in 'see', but I gather it's the publican with a few drinks in his system just checking ID. No drama; I'm twenty-four, but people do say I look younger. I search through my little brown carryall and pull out my licence. The photo of me was taken three years ago, when I was a very different person to today. Blonde-tipped hair, thin cheeks, a smile. My hair is now thick, brown, long and ringleted. My face has disappeared into a flabby cushion and my smile has been absorbed by my pancreas. I hope the publican can't see the difference in this light.

I timidly walk over to the group of men in my drab, size 24 clothes. No one is talking now. They're all wearing office clothes but the evening has undone their top buttons, revealing skin where their ties should be. A man who I assume is the publican steps forward and takes my licence. He squints at it and hands it back. 'It's a woman!'

The group hold up their beers and cheer. I'm in shock. The man puts his hand on my crotch to verify my licence and they all laugh and drink.

I run out of Nine Cats and never go into another pub. Instead, I drink at home. I unearth friendly-looking heroin addicts on the route to the bottle shop and invite them back to my flat. They inject, throw up on my carpet, steal my treasures and come round at all hours, accompanied by other strangers. I'm too useless to stop it.

My only meaningful human interaction is with my mental health caseworkers. 'How are you.' 'Is the medication working.' 'Do you need a new script.' Never with a question mark. 'Okay,' I say to each not-question. I've replaced beer with tranquillisers because pills are cheaper and far more portable than slabs of beer. My modus operandi is to collect valium and diazepam scripts from different doctors around town. It's hard to judge how many pills to take when I take them all the time, but the handful gets bigger as my body keeps adapting. I start to overdose because that dreamless kind of sleep is far more satisfying than the medical coma the antipsychotics put me in. I somehow have enough sense of self-preservation to take myself to the emergency department, where the doctor puts charcoal through my gut and I lie half asleep in the company of other human beings who are actually sick. A doctor always finishes off by asking me if I was serious. My answer is always no, I don't want to die, it's just that life is not working. Because I answer no, I walk out of the ED every time.

One day or night, I emerge from a deep foggy moor on my lounge room floor to find a woman standing beside me. I recognise her. She's a patient from the psych rehab group, but I don't know why she's in my house: she's not a drug user. I pass out. When I wake up again, I'm in a hospital bed with a needle in my arm and the taste of charcoal in my mouth. She later tells me angrily that I rang her to say that this was the biggie, goodbye. She leaves my life with the advice: 'If you're going to kill yourself, next time do it properly.'

My whole life revolves around getting pills, over-dosing and waking up. I'm juggling three collapsing time zones, and being awake is sending out flares to every psyche bounty hunter there is. I need to stop waking up. I overdose on the benzos again. I'm found and taken to hospital by someone, I don't know who or where or when. This time, instead of getting up and staggering out as per the usual routine—'Were you serious?' 'No'—the hospital admits me back to the psych ward. I'm pushed in through the one-way door. I look around at the familiar fish tank and see all the plastic seaweed and the pirate's treasure chest in the corner opening and closing, letting out bubbles of air, and the funny little fish floating around with no energy to swim, and I'm done.

Despite it all, or perhaps because of it, I believe in God. His plans for Earth mean that while creatures are technically alive, they are required to breathe. I have to make a choice. Either lie down and stay in here forever, gulping bubbles of piped air and flopping around just for the sake of some form of movement, or climb up the edges and play the game of respiring freely. I choose up. My ancestral suspicion kicks in over the top of Saxon gloom and says this is not how it needs to be. I need to get on my feet, feel the earth below and see the space above. But if I am to get anywhere, first I have to find a light. A real, shining, useful light. Not a bloody big torch illuminating my drowned face.

EVENT HORİZON

IF I COULD WAVE A wand and make that whole school
vanish, leaving me with just my imaginary horses and
quantifiable nature, I would've been happy living out
that story for the rest of my life. But out of the blue,
when I was nine, my parents plucked me, my brother
and baby sister out of obscurity and repotted us in
Australia.

Mum and Dad spent all the money they made from
the sale of their cottage on buses, aeroplanes, trains and
taxis. We flew out of London with one suitcase each
and an exuberant anticipation of adventure. Our time in
Perth was short-lived as the last flicker of Dad's savings
dwindled on a spectacular hotel room overlooking
the Swan River. Our skylord for two marvellous days
evicted us with a ceremonial spraying of disinfectant

and fifteen minutes to get out. A very long shiny train took us across the Nullarbor to Adelaide, and as funds rapidly decreased, so did the quality of our transport and accommodation. The long shiny train with individual beds and washbowls gave way to a short, rickety noisy train with benches for seats and a single toilet for the whole carriage.

For the next few months, we bunkered down in migrant hostels in Melbourne until Dad had saved enough from his factory job for a mortgage. Without flicking through a street directory, Mum spun a compass and found north in a three-bedroom brick-veneer house in the stinking-hot concrete slab of a suburb called Doveton. We moved in with five suitcases and an electric kettle, sleeping on camp beds borrowed from nuns and eating McDonald's every other night for supper. It was great fun.

Doveton sounds like there should be tonnes of doves, but there were none. It was more like a derelict cage of ravens, vultures and doomed carrion, landlocked by social tectonics of post-war bulimia. The suburb up to every horizon in every direction revealed itself to be a coal-powered grimy network of factories and cardboard commission houses, held together by sinews of far-flung immigrants trying to start a new life in an old town with no money. I was as far, far away from the folk of oak trees, foxes and snowy winters, as possible. To get my head around this new land, I needed to transpose my former life with this new one and begin to reset my bearings.

Luckily for me and my brother, Mum and Dad held on to their love of the idyllic Celtic countryside and found a house next to the as-yet-unknown floodplain paddocks of Dandenong Creek. Like in St Weonards, our new house stood alongside a farm, but it didn't look or smell as nice because—it was later revealed—before the housing estate was built, the place was the council tip. Soil had been laid over the top, but bits of bright blue plastic now poked up through the grass and stuck out of cow pats, and old car parts and sculptures of twisted rusted metal entwined with blackberry bushes seeped up from the earth as if floating to the surface of a dried-out sea. A permanent pong of mouldy earth hung low in the air, tingeing sweet cooking and washing smells with an odour of dead dirt. The kids in my street taught me to say 'paddock' instead of 'field', but for a long time the word filled me with existential dread. It invoked the image of a ruddy old farmer battling with

'Old car parts and sculptures of twisted rusted
metal entwined with blackberry bushes.'

a big slimy fish until, listening to 'Nightlife' on the ABC many years later, I learned the word 'paddock' is a derivative of the Scottish word 'park'—roll the *r* and you get paddock. What relief.

No one thinks of English immigrants needing to relearn English, but I had a phobia of saying the words *grass*, *pool* and *garage* at my new primary school in Doveton for a long time. I was terrified of anything that would cause someone to reach into my schoolbag and pull out the real me from St Weonards, and saying these words wrong drew curious hands over. I worked extra hard to make sure my face was as free of visible mucus as possible—which was very difficult due to perpetual hay fever, but not impossible once I worked out a system of timed distraction so I could snort back the glacier before anyone noticed. Those names must not follow me.

Living for almost a year without a family bathroom of our own taught me a good lesson in managing my own hygiene in public. I was no longer able to sit quietly in damp pants all day because of the constant proximity to: a) my mum; b) 500 other people; and c) my suitcase with ten more pairs. My worldly travels had given me a sliver of confidence and the first time I put my hand up in class to ask to go to the toilet felt like a huge accomplishment. I was immensely proud. At this new school, 15,000 kilometres away from the hell of my St Weonards school, I was determined to have a fresh go at being me. At this school, I wouldn't be prey. It wasn't too challenging, because I soon came to realise Doveton was a collective of bullied kids.

Apart from the stress of navigating the language, I was excited to be exploring the new southern earth around my house with the same gusto as my earlier era, even if there were snakes and spiders with red backs that murdered people. None of these were in my pre-installed compendium of fear—the Devil, UFOs, the Old Man and the Witch—so I wasn't bothered by them. My biggest regret was not owning one of the unkempt ponies that roamed through the tall grass on the other side of our fence. They seemed ownerless and carried galactic burrs in their tangled manes, which I happily pulled out with my yearning fingers. I had grown half-a-metre in height since the riding school; the ponies no longer looked down on me.

Then, when I turned sixteen, something glorious happened. My aunt died and left me $800. After a decade of pestering, Mum gave in and said I could buy a horse, which I'm sure gave her a flash of childhood joy too. Together we looked at a few random horses for sale through *The Trading Post* before settling on a grey horse called Bobbi because he came with all the gear, including a saddle. By now, I was working in a casual job shelving books at the local library, but it wasn't enough to pay for Bobbi's upkeep and agistment. With a few phone calls to the owner of the farm next door, though, we struck a deal whereby I was able to keep Bobbi in the paddock for free on the condition that he would be used by the Riding for the Disabled program on weekdays.

Bobbi quickly let us know he was half Cupid, half demon. When the sun was out and birds were singing, he was a rocking horse, adorable, obedient and polite. But if the wind shifted and a cloud passed over the sun, his blood thickened and his eyes would blow up into giant red mushrooms. His head thrashed about and his hooves became horns, ramming at the dirt as if it were the head of Satan coming straight at him. I could only imagine what it would be like for the disabled rider should the sun go behind a cloud. But to my surprise he continued to be used, so I wondered if it was all a filthy trick he played only on me so that I would let him go back to grazing in the paddock.

I started out with Bobbi a complete novice, wearing a brand-new white Stack Hat and sitting up straight like I'd been taught at riding school. But as Doveton soaked in, my English-ness leaked out. The helmet came off, one hand let go of the reins, my back rounded. As I improved, my battles with Bobbi lessened. Where once he had bucked me from his back with a mimimum of effort, when he found it required more energy, he gave up. During school holidays, Bobbi and I headed out through the paddocks, going further along the creek each time. I knew I was at my horseriding pinnacle when I smoked a cigarette with my free hand.

I started to hang out with a few local kids volunteering at the farm and we spent days out there with the RDA horses and swimming in the thick sludgy Dandenong Creek, much to Mum's disgust. Her fastidiously clean washing already smelled like the tip; she didn't need more help. The creek was often described in the newspaper as toxic, but teenagers are immune to everything, so the look, taste and smell meant nothing but disobedient fun. I was learning heaps.

In late winter, massive floods came up to our fence, trapping cows on mounds of old rubbish, and the creek flew like a flock of mad emus. The murky, grey water spread out for miles across the paddocks; only the constant violent flip-flapping of tea-tree tops gave any clue to the whereabouts of the actual creek. Up near the farm, the creek sucked back in every ounce of wild water and slammed it together down the concrete culvert under the Kidds Road bridge. It was an awesome sight and the sound drowned out any conversation.

It was here that two boys I knew from the farm tied a long rope around a girl's waist and told her to get into the fuming water. They'd already asked me to do it, because I seemed to be the first picked to do anything dangerous, for some reason I hadn't yet worked out, but there was no way I was going anywhere near that insane washing machine. So instead they offered the gig to the pretty girl who every boy wanted. She had more to prove. None of them had figured out what would happen after this point, so they were surprised when, as soon as she jumped in, she immediately disappeared under the bridge in a torrent of raging grey water. Life was on her side, fortunately, and the boys held tight to the rope, tying it around a tree trunk in a moment of clarity. Instead of pulling the girl in, though, they gleefully waved at her to go further, because people were on the bridge watching the 'show'.

Dandenong Creek swallowed at least four people in the years we poked it. One was a well-liked farm volunteer and horsey person who'd gone out rounding up ducks for the night to save them from the foxes. We found his boots and socks neatly bundled on the bank next to the creek, and his soggy old Akubra caught up in some rocks below. The police divers found him the next day and I watched as his sodden black-shirted back surfaced, breaking the muddy brown water like a big turtle coming up for air, but not taking a breath even when it was clear the turtle should take one. The sight of his saturated dead body ricocheted like lightning down to my feet and thundered back up to my mind, somehow reminding me of treacherous days yet to come. The creek, the farm, the bridge—everything collided here.

My little patch of blue sky, unscathed by storms, was Bobbi. He was the perfect pillow for teenage tears; his grey fur soaked me up without getting wet and his brown jellybean eyes held all the sadness and joy mine were losing. When I was angry we galloped up into the hills, when I was reckless we jumped fallen trees, and we splashed through lingering floods when I was frustrated. In return, I ventured out into freezing, blustery nights to put a rug on him when a cold change came through unexpectedly. I didn't stop to consider how lucky I was. It didn't occur to me that it all might be a fleeting life memory I should etch into the pith of my mind. I just lived in every moment with my horse; the map of his being, the routine of gear, the ingrained knowledge of movement, the freedom of desire paths. I devoured every inch of his country, learning the shades of nuance in his air, water, plants and soil.

～

Hints of an adult future started to emerge through the scrub. Being around nature so much, I eventually decided it was time to make it official. There was a perfect job I'd seen on telly; it had stuck in my mind like one of those grass burrs and itched me every time I brushed past it. I decided I would leave school in year ten and become a ranger. I could mix my love of the outdoors with my penchant for gathering useful information. (I was growing into a bit of a know-all, but know-alls need a willing audience and Doveton

'I just lived in every moment with my horse;
the map of his being.'

was not a town for know-alls, as it put a bullseye on your forehead for know-nothings.)

Dirt under my nails had become so much more appealing to me than nail polish on top. In fact, it had cured me from sucking on my two middle fingers well into my teens. As far back as my very early memories of the rugged Welsh border countryside, nature was the only society I could handle. It operated slower and more meaningfully that that of people, and it gave me time to converse in a language that didn't involve listening to voices and speaking in mine. I loved the code of trees, dirt and clouds and, like any student linguist, I wanted to understand the grammar and syntax to be able to communicate fully. It wasn't good enough for me to say, 'What a beautiful view'; I wanted to acknowledge what made it beautiful and what constituted a view.

As I meandered through high school to year ten, the only subject that piqued my interest, apart from art, was geology. I was surprised that it was even a subject with all the words and numbers going on. Rocks and stones got under my skin when I went on some fossicking trips with Dad. On one expedition to a huge limestone quarry outside Geelong, I unearthed a three-million-year-old shark's tooth and carried it around in my pencil case until it snapped in half. I didn't give a thought to its human value.

Subterranean nature impressed me as much as that above. A metamorphic igneous rock was equal parts awe-inspiring and mundane; it had been spewed out of a gazillion-degree volcano erupting with molten lava from thousands of miles underground and yet sat so placidly in my hand as a cold, old, boring rock. The only other time I felt this tug and pull of big and small was encountering a large silver UFO up close with my brother back in Wales one misty, snow-laden evening. Seeing it sweep across the sky just above the garden treetops with noticeable purpose opened the book in my mind to the unique matter of time and space. The graceful but terrifying sight set my perpetual curiosity in motion to work out how a machine so big and heavy could travel through the air so perfectly lightly and quietly. The experience fed into radiating episodes of panic that seeped into the fate of mental illness, but also introduced me to a frequency of colour that can't be accessed by many people who thrive in the middle bit.

Unfortunately, my plan to leave high school and take up a ranger traineeship with the Department of Sustainability and Environment (now known as

Department of Sticks and Embers) didn't accord with my parents' plan; they had decreed that I would be the first person in my family to finish high school in Australia. It was hard to fight their earnest intent; Dad worked long hours at the factory to send me to a Catholic high school. So I sadly watched the traineeship trickle away into the bush without taking me with it.

I spent another two years at that school learning how to buy two tomatoes for the price of a potato, and being dragged kicking and screaming through English. My final results:

Practical maths: 51%
English: D
Art: Pass
Geology: A+
Socialising: epic fail.

Towards the end of my school life, I was just an impression. My identity was dying. I wafted to school, floated into class and wafted home afterwards. There were no solid social walls or concrete human floors for me to hold on to and give me a sense of proven self. I did manage to make a couple of friends, but only one at a time, as it was hard for me to process the relationship, and it completely stressed me out if that friend had other friends. I couldn't fathom the matrix. I tried and tried to mould my body into the shape of other humans around me. I yearned to be like them and copied their likes in popular music and clothes, even though the patterned, pleated fabric made me itchy and angry, and the faces of the celebrities on the posters on my wall looked down at me with prying, bossy eyes, judging me on my failure to come up with my own crush.

It's so much easier for the universe to break apart than it is to keep things together. The pavements around Doveton were full of cracks and the worn-out people who moved jarringly along them only stirred the dust. My legs and feet worked fine, so my reward was that I walked to and from school every day, even through hailstorms and torrential rain. The constant dampness never dried, though, because it often rained so hard at home, and sometimes lightning struck, burning up my clothes altogether. I had nowhere to hang out my belongings to dry and become warm. It was only a matter of time before my increasingly heavy footprints drew the attention of those who were in the business of noticing heavy footprints.

On my regular passage through the cracking pavements on the way to and from school in my dark green uniform and blazer, I was often harassed by my fellow teenage Dovetonites without the luxury of such nauseating green garnish. It got even worse when I started to ride my new Christmas bike to school. On the positive side, my teachers made it known that I was the first female ever to ride a bike to school in De La Salle history. On the negative side, apparently it was hilarious to see a girl in a long tweed skirt, brown tights and a horse rug of a blazer riding a bicycle. Pedalling home tenaciously one afternoon despite the accompanying ditty about riding home on my pushbike, honey, an innovative newly formed group of kids one block away from home decided to throw stones at me. I weighed up the options and decided a ten-minute bike ride with three minutes of rocks was far less traumatic than an hour-long trudge on foot, still with the possibility of rocks.

I rode home through the asteroid belt every day for a few weeks until, out of nowhere, a small group of miscellaneous warriors sprang out of the hedges and ambushed the rock throwers with bigger rocks, telling them they were big fat cunts. Surprising myself—and

'I rode home through the asteroid belt every day.'

despite the shock of hearing the word 'cunt'—I jumped off my bike and joined the fray; it only seemed right. The rock throwers ran off and I was left standing on the street corner with my gritty godlike saviours. They looked like any other kids in the area, so I asked them why they'd peformed such an act of heroism for me. A tall blond boy with a John Farnham haircut and smile to match replied that those puny wankers had it coming. It seemed they had some kind of score to settle and I was as good as a tennis net. I don't think they expected the tennis net to throw itself into the game, but it did.

Judging by their ability to materialise anywhere except near a schoolbag, my new friends either didn't want to go to school or just bypassed the concept. But their disdain for authority synced effortlessly with mine and I quickly fell from my perch in the rusty cage onto the grit paper of life on the streets. How quickly it can happen. The feeling of being one of the team, and someone thinking I was worth fighting for, was divine. There was no way I was going to let that feeling go. The cool kids at school now seemed childish and naive with their short, short school skirts, talking back to teachers and smoking cigarettes down the oval at lunchtime. I was with the *really* cool kids.

I left my bike on the corner and followed the streets around to the side and found all sorts of curious things there, like a coconut bong and a spray can. On tentative forays around the event horizon, I dropped all sorts of clues for my teachers—the only adults in my life capable of rescuing me—that I was dangerously near a dead sun. I wanted them to see that I was tumbling out into an abyss of no return but I didn't know how to show them. So I sat on the footpath outside school until dusk, huddled up against the school fence, watching as teachers streamed out of the car park, hoping that just one would look over, stop and ask if I was alright. Surely my wretched presence looked odd? But not one teacher saw me despite the many times I tried. Like the influencers in the psych ward to come, those with power were only interested in the vulnerable who gave some kind of payback, not the ones like me who had the gravitational waves of a pebble. With Mum and Dad hopelessly lost in Australia and my sense of self vanishing in the dust, the streets gave me the sonic boom a young person needed, so I went with it.

Like the language of trees and soil, the language of the streets is sublime. It's real. It has its own time. Nothing matters apart from matter. As with all my interests, I gave 100 per cent of my attention to this new reality and easily picked up useful information, becoming a fluent speaker of the culture within months. Yet unlike many of the people around me, I never volunteered my body to the cultural practices; it participated by association. Within one rotation of my new planet around the sun, my skin and mind were a blackberry bush of bruises, scars and nightmares, but they were medals I wore with dark pride.

The early exhilarating sense that I was a respected team member soon turned into the inescapable realisation that I was entertainment. My mind might've wanted to play along with this new game, but my body and brain had other ideas. I didn't have the authentic skills required to be a street person. I was too nice and obliging. Because of my inability to process drugs and brain damage very well, they gave me a name based on my character—Blob. As Blob, I couldn't tie my shoelaces or hold a cup of coffee. I gave stoned people hours of fun with witty drunken commentary and my ability to walk into poles and—with innate comedic timing—into potholes. Yet I was tormented with threats of rape because I didn't know how to have sex. I was the first to try pills, powder and pinpricks. If I didn't, there would be air in the needle and a knife to the throat. If I didn't, the silenced teasing from primary school would reappear and finish me off me with spiteful glee. Even through all this, I still preferred identity.

Eventually the sweet little stone-throwing kids I met on the street corner growing pot and playing with needles, VB and petrol melted back into the bushes and resurfaced as adults with scrolls and maps charting the whereabouts of everything. These people were the same age as me, but were serious business people. They kept fastidious calendars to know when and where to access 'free' lawnmowers and chainsaws, and we sat around spoon tables not coffee tables to discuss the day's events. My presence was of no more value to this set than the dog they kept chained in the backyard.

Once drawn into this orbit, I had no means of escape. I'd gone from Blob to Lump. They sucked me into places I didn't want to go but my mind and arms were too broken to fight. I didn't understand I was the bottom rung in a minority, but the ladder went downwards not up. I didn't know life didn't have to feel like a constant series of momentous decisions. I didn't realise I could say no, I could walk away, that I could trust in my instincts that this field was not mine to master. Nothing revealed to me there were vast numbers of people out there doing far more wonderful, joyous everyday things that didn't involve surviving dying every day. I didn't know life wasn't meant to be like this.

The memories of that universe pulsate with wild flames in my eyes and the thick gunpowder dust of the last battle still thickens the air as I sit here in the psych ward, thinking.

'He holds a guitar to his love-starved chest and
his fingers point to places on the strings.'

THE OLD MAN
AND THE GUITAR

THE OLD MAN SITS IN the Frankston psych rehab music
group, seemingly irrelevant. His face is pulled down
with invisible weights; his body is thin and gnarled like
the final leaf on a dying tree in a drought. He holds a
guitar to his love-starved chest and his fingers point
to places on the strings. With a small flurry of atoms,
his hands begin to twinkle. Music wells up from his
core and spreads across the room in ribbons of slow
motion lightning. His music is very different to the
strained cat noise that we suffer through every second
Wednesday—where we all moan along to Beatles songs,
pretending to enjoy ourselves, while inside we're all
geniuses who could solve world hunger if we were in
the UN Creative Discussion rehab group instead of
this music group.

This music, it's royal. Something in me goes 'ping' and I feel my heart fill as if it has just connected to a missing part. Everyone in the room is listening with heads tilted, eyes awakened. The old man keeps playing without visible fear. We only see the top of his tatty old hat; his bobbing head is down, almost covering his hands, and it's clear he's absorbed in his project. The music is a simple melody yet it unfurls a huge map in my headspace, touching every synapse laneway and firing every neuron alley.

Serenade completed, he puts the guitar aside. He looks up and reveals a gnarled, pockmarked face, old but youthful. Thin grey strands of half-hair trickle from under his cap. His body betrays deep embarrassment yet his humanity allows himself to accept little nibbles of praise proffered by those who can. We all know it's the best music we've heard in this room. The staff give one side of their face to congratulations, yet I see the other side is shady with disdain. How dare Andrés Segovia interrupt their music therapy!

The room empties and the therapist forgets to put the guitar back in the safe. It leans benignly against the far wall and I have an urge to approach it. When everyone is gone, I sidle over and pick it up. It feels weird. I'm aware I'm holding something so precious, so sacred, without the permission to do so, but the guitar seems willing. I sit on the floor and try to wrangle my lumpy hands into the shape of the old man's dancing hands. It's awkward. I gather that guitars are like horses and judge a person in a millisecond of contact. It must now hate me. I pray that no one can see me and report my belligerent thought of smashing it. I persevere with fumbling fingers until we reach our first treaty and a single clear note emanates. I make a commitment to the universe that I will do everything I can to learn the language of the guitar. In return, it will be a kind and patient instrument that will allow me into its world. We will be friends, I know.

～

I'm released from the psych ward much like the first time, but more quickly because of my ability in psychiatrian language—or it could be the government's new approach to mental health, which declares the average psych ward stay to be six weeks. It's amazing how they can now cure all mental patients in six weeks. But unlike last time, I have a mission that doesn't involve cheese rings. I want to play guitar. I hear music in my head. All sorts of music—orchestras, opera singers, crooners, punks, sweet folk singers, rap. I enjoy hearing my music; it's exclusive and entertaining in the lonely hours. But I writhe in agony when I hear the discombobulated opera singer! I can't stand opera. The sound makes my brain vibrate and feels like knives cutting into parts of my skull. The guitar will be the perfect tool to turn my own special music into outside music. It's okay to have your own personal radio station, but it would be even better if other people could dial in too.

I find a music shop in town and, with a bit of guidance from the owner, purchase a Valencia full-sized student classical guitar. He assures me it's easier on the fingertips to learn on a nylon-string guitar rather than one with steel strings. To help my project along, I create a new destination away from the bottle shop: the library. I borrow every book on music I can find. I'm not a great reader, but over the course of a year I manage to trawl through books on music theory; on guitars, chords, lyrics, songwriting, singing and harmonies; on music of the spheres and music of the years; on how the brain processes music; on how music was invented; and on how music has helped people to survive wars, tragedies, disasters, prison and trauma. I teach myself Mozart and

'I borrow every book on music I can find.'

Beethoven; the Eagles, Fleetwood Mac and the Beatles. I strum new chords to accompany my special music, notating it all on manuscript paper. I begin to sing and am very happy that my voice is in tune with my music.

Apart from a series of lessons involving scales and simple children's songs on an old piano when I was about twelve, I've never had formal music lessons. I wanted to sing in high school musicals, but my quiet voice betrayed me. The school would put out a call for students to audition to sing in *The Wizard of Oz* or *A Christmas Carol*, and every year I would quietly teach myself the audition song while walking home from school in the wind, the rain, the beating sun, the hail and thunder. And every year the teachers would tell me to look up and sing a bit louder, and every year I would sing about a quarter of a decibel louder and look further into my shoes, and every year the teacher would say, 'Sorry, you're just too quiet. We can't hear you.'

I would walk out of the audition room feeling as pathetic as the hole in my brown sock. I didn't have any friends, I struggled to fit in, and my only talents were for losing my temper and drawing horses. None of that was of any good to anyone. I needed to sing; I just didn't know how to. I didn't think I was allowed to.

One day in year eleven, all the popular kids were setting up a fashion show in the lecture theatre and I was feeling a bit arrogant, so I walked in to watch while I ate my lunch. There was a microphone standing all alone down the front of the stage while the fashionable students fussed and flurried around with their giant egos on the stage behind it. It suddenly looked compelling because I felt its strange loneliness. It seemed to be asking me to help it do its thing. It reminded me of an eager dog holding up a stick, saying, 'C'mon, throw it! I don't care who you are or where you're from. I don't care that no one likes you or that they think you're weird. Just throw the stick. We'll have fun!'

Because the other students were so busy, I thought they wouldn't notice too much if I went up to the microphone and said something into it. I was shaking as I walked over to it, but the microphone was pulling me into its orbit. I couldn't resist. It was strange for me to do something so courageous and subversive. Increasing noise from the streets and the fluctuating shift in power dynamics at home was altering my 'give-a-damn' quota.

Understandably, Mum and Dad weren't prepared for the giant leap in consciousness their children would experience when shifting furniture 15,000 kilometres to the right within twenty-four hours. Suddenly here we were, completely unhitched from any past and future. Back there, in the dark, I was a lonesome child wandering around a remote rural village, playing with clouds and singing with wind whispers. Here, in the light, I was a lonely semi-adult, looking for any friends to show me how to move my bones around their space and shape my tongue around their words.

Time moved with us. My unexpected progress into adolescence apparently not only broke my parents' hearts, it also broke the chain of a well-worn ancestral habit. I got good at being angry. I thought later that maybe I had too much testosterone, because I woke up with a face covered in seething pimples and with another metre added to my height. I yelled at Mum and Mum yelled back. Same with Dad, except his yelling came with a cautionary film rating. The new baby screamed for three years straight. We were just trying to hear each other over the noise. Mum suffered from one long migraine, and Dad worked and worked and worked in a metal-bending factory to cope with the noise and tension at home.

Every contract I held with the universe was being torn up and thrown into a raging fire. My travel-shocked parents seemed like they wanted to shrink space, calcifying a familiar view from the kitchen window. Noise roared in my head whenever I tripped over my own stupid body trying to fit my curvaceous soul back into this cube at the end of each day. Outside the front door, I was terrified of being seen, heard or thought about because I didn't know what part of my brain to activate to deal with eye contact or whereabouts in the mind I should put sadness or happiness invoked by other people.

My coping skills became the darkened depths at the back of my wardrobe or curled up in a tiny ball behind the ugly green vinyl chair in the bathroom where I stayed unmoving for hours, no one knowing where the breath of my life was being drawn and released. I liked that feeling of compression and disappearance. My other skill was etching out bloodlines on my arms, telling the story of pain which my voice was unable.

The two opposing forces at home created energy that rippled out across the universe, bounced off the far edges and came back, landing in me as dark matter. My soul was constantly shaking. Waves of resentment, shame, judgement, revenge and shock had built up to the point where my year eleven audition was a perfect place to experiment with my overwhelming feeling of Fuck Them, Fuck Me and Fuck You. No big crinkle in fabric goes unnoticed by fabric.

I put my mouth up to the funny-looking silver-mesh ball. It was cold and prickly when my lip accidentally brushed it. I adjusted my stance, raised my eyes up towards the empty rows of seats at the top of the theatre and started singing the chorus of a song that I liked. The sound of my voice came out loud, strong and perfectly in tune. With the extra volume, I even held the end note and trilled it a little to make it reverberate in the acoustic universe I could feel opening up in the theatre. I felt in control of the world like I'd never felt before, as if nothing was wrong anywhere.

I'd never heard my voice like this before and it surprised me as much as the other people in the theatre. 'Who gave you permission to use that microphone?' one of the girls screeched from behind me. 'Get away from it!' another snarled. Two or three of them came bustling at me like I'd touched their golden jewellery. I felt ashamed, small and ugly again, so I grabbed the rest of my precious ham sandwich and disappeared into obscurity among the sleepwalkers who were waiting in the wings.

"Who gave you permission to use that microphone?"

But now, with this guitar, I once again have the power to create my own music in my own home with no group of bossy spoiled brats in sight. I am in control once more. No one can tell me to stop or move away from my songs. The only negative feedback is from the poor people in the flat next to mine, who yell at me through the wall to stop playing 'She'll Be Coming Round the Mountain'. They have every right to complain. I've been playing it over and over every day for almost a year. I need to get my left hand used to changing chords from C to G to F with absolute precision.

I busk in the main street of Frankston, playing classical music. Despite my phobia of being looked at, I get looked at. Classical music and Frankston are not a well-known combination, but I earn little bits of money from a few clandestine followers. Instead of buying beer, I buy a cup of coffee. Instead of eating a box of Cheezels, I play Bach's 'Air on the G String' ten times. When I cry, the top edge of the guitar collects my tears as they drip drip drip down onto the polished wood. I wake every morning and the guitar is still there. It wasn't a dream after all! It becomes a constant, safe, trustworthy ally. In contrast to nearly every single

'I busk in the main street of Frankston,

playing classical music.'

human I've known, this friend isn't out to hurt me (unless I count excruciating pain on my fingertips) and wants nothing more than to be loved. After an obsessive twelve months of strumming, plucking, humming and forming tough, dead skin on the tips of my fingers, I can play guitar. This is the reliable floor I needed to stand on and the music, a shining light guiding me on. I finally have hope. The old man with a guitar was my true saviour.

I venture out into a new land and suddenly the fox is there, watching. Can you see him? Maybe not—he's clever at hiding.

THE FOX

WITHOUT WARNING, FOX LEAPS OUT from under the heath back into the risk of daylight. His head is as low as his spine. His beautiful flaming tail follows him like a second animal caught up in his vortex of speed. For a dreamy split second, he thinks he might be safe there in the prickly bush. But the growing mountain of noise from the baying dogs and the braying Men spark his instinct to get out of there fast. A fox never assumes safety. As he springs forward, his front paw lands heavily on a prickle and he yelps in pain. But he allows himself no time for self-pity. A momentary thorn now will be a life-ending crown of daggers if he doesn't keep moving.

Fox grew up in this scrub. His father was a quiet authority, only giving Fox the protection he needed to

Map of Fox

'As a pup, Fox learned his ways by doing and
remembered by rote. He studied every rise and fall
of the ground, every bend in the nearby stream,
until he no longer had to think about it.'

get through his first six weeks. He was gone a lot, so Fox spent most of his infancy with his mother in the earth. She made sure the den was sheltered from the wind, rain and heat, and brought just enough food for them to share. They were a tight-knit family and never welcomed strangers into their company. These billowy lands had been in their family territory for decades. Fox knew the ground well.

As a pup, Fox learned his ways by doing and remembered by rote. He studied every rise and fall of the ground, every bend in the nearby stream, until he no longer had to think about it. His mother vixen showed him where to fill up with fatty protein in the bounteous spring and where a sticky cricket could be sprung in the desperate ends of a dusty summer. He watched with her as the evenings rolled in through the long tussocks near their earth and learned when it was safe to go out for the night. They ventured as far as human earth on the east, west and south. The north border was a huge riotous track, always filled with dangerous, noisy and angry creatures constantly marking their territory. These shiny animals were a mystery to Fox. If a careless field animal strayed onto their patch of hard earth, those vicious beasts with the weird feet would mercilessly slay the poor lost soul, leaving its pulped body at the side of the track as a dire warning to others.

Fox also knew the sound of Men. These human creatures did a lot of obvious tramping and trudging with much carrying on. Fox understood that humans were unable to see or hear very well, because they usually missed simple warnings about a lot of things that Fox thought very important, like a hole in the ground or a torrential downpour coming. He assumed that Men's sense of smell was far keener than his, however, as they always managed to scout out their prey. He accepted that Men sat on a throne at the top of the food pyramid.

This system was a simple agreement made a very long time ago when some modest animals decided they wanted to be clothed in fur rather than parade around naked. The agreement was signed off on, but came with a condition—to be clothed in fur, these animals had to take the fur from other animals. To respect the victim's dignity, their naked body would go back into the earth.

With their short fluffy tails as hats on their head, Men were part of this contract. Men ate foxes (why else would they kill them?) so, like any furry target, Fox had to learn escape tactics from a very early age. That basically involved swift running and clever manoeuvres. Most of the time Men were very good at the game. Any unlucky target had to employ every trick in the Book of Fox to survive this master killing machine. But most of the time, foxes and humans managed to live in lopsided harmony. Men threw a lot of good food away and that was beneficial to Fox and his family.

It was a late autumn evening and Fox was almost a year old. He and his mother vixen were watching the sun lay its glorious soul back into the ground when Mother suggested it was time for Fox to leave their earth. He was now wise enough to try out his living skills alone. They'd both known this time was coming, so they'd enjoyed a gentle and forgiving farewell over the summer months. Every time the family went to hunt, Fox ventured a little further and stayed out a little later. Sometimes he slept in his own earth and came home just as the sun was waking. Fox gradually began to understand that he no longer needed his mother's earth.

And so he went away with all the best training in the world to find his own earth. For this next stage of life, he spent every waking hour practising his skills of invisibility as he crept through the fields of slow Cow.

If he made a mistake, tripped on a log or tangled himself in a wire, Cow would look up, causing all cows to look up. As all cows do. Then Fox would admonish himself for being clumsy. If he got to the other side of the field with not so much as an ear wiggle from Cow, then he praised himself for his superpowers. But he never got too proud. Never stopped too long to eat and drink. He knew the risk of letting his senses become lazy. In the wild, you must assume there's always another pair of eyes, another hungry mouth that you haven't seen.

A farmer has seen Fox near his chicken, and Fox—thoroughly focused on his own occupation—didn't see Man watching him. It was a momentary oversight and now Fox is running for his life. The dogs let out piercing joyful screams and there's loud language that Fox can't understand, though he knows its intent. Although Fox wants to, he can't stop the game and explain to Man that he is starving. The winter months have been very hard on his belly. Fox had reasoned that as he was lower than Man in the food chain, and if Chicken was even *lower*, then that clucky squawky bird must therefore be fair game to them both. This is the way in the wild surely.

Fox sprints on. He's tired but still expertly snakes through tree and over fallen branch. His perfect stride is quick and confident but his energy is starting to wane. He eventually skids on a corner and slams into a thick tree trunk. His eyes see nothing for a few moments and his head pounds with the force in his blood. He needs a better plan. Think, Fox, think!

Man is fast. His dogs are faster. Foxes are fast too, but the ground is getting smaller. He can't run forever. Men's dogs are very efficient at picking up a scent and they share Fox's ability to read the ground at speed. There must be a solution to all these problems. As he thinks, the sound of the hunt picks up. No time, no time! Wait. There is one last thing to try. Fox knows the north border is nearby, full of dangerous creatures that even Men do not go near. They are fast too, faster than Men. With all the energy he can muster, Fox takes off north towards the fastest animals on the planet.

At the edge of the precipice, Fox pauses. With the leanest side-to-side glance, his speeding brain calculates the basic physics of the track of illogical animals crisscrossing in front of his wild eyes. His next move will either grant his life, or allow an ugly but concluding end.

Either way, the dogs are so close behind him now, they have full view of their prey. Fox has no time to decide. He flexes his lithe body and leaps onto the crazy track. A gnarling monster bellows into his right ear. He narrowly slides past it and straight into the gaping jaw of another. He jumps sideways hard. The sounds are deafening but he can't stop now. His feet work fast, many times faster than they ever worked in the field of Cow. A square-eyed beast ploughs down hard on his left side. Another appears from a belch of choking black smoke. Fox steps back, then lunges forward like a spring. He's made it halfway. A miracle.

Fox's world is now full of horrid screeching, banging, belching noises that scream through his senses. Yet the monsters still haven't managed to stomp on him. He takes heart and makes one last hope-filled dash to the other side. In a blur of colour and sound, Fox breaks free of the hellish track and feels the soft ground beneath his sore, tired feet. Without time to say a prayer of thanks to his Maker, Fox now runs as fast as he possibly can with all the strength left in his body. Run, Fox. Just run. He focuses his gaze on the furthest horizon. He imagines he has big silver wings on his back and they give him extra speed and agility. For the first time,

'Yet the monsters still haven't managed to stomp on him.'

Fox doesn't hear dogs or Men behind. He is free. The risk has paid off.

The Men and their dogs stopped at the edge of the trail of angry beasts. Except they know it as the six-lane Princes Highway. It was extra busy at that particular time of day with people coming home from work in the city and day trips to the country. The Men have great visions of the fox smashed out dead in the wake of a semitrailer. Even without actually witnessing this gruesome carnage, the thought is gratification. They call back the swirling pack of dogs and return in a leisurely manner to farms on the eastern fringes of suburbia. 'No more trouble from that bloody vermin,' is the closing statement. The dogs pretend to rip each other apart to satisfy their excited unsated teeth.

Go, Fox, go. Enjoy your freedom!

'Go, Fox, go. Enjoy your freedom!'

ANÎMUS

I GREW UP IN FOX country. The wintery edges of the Welsh countryside, fed by regular downpours, and the unkempt weathered paddocks of Doveton with the stinky creek running through both provided abundant hidey-holes for foxes to evade the vindictive gaze of humans. Only the occasional telltale flash of red suggested hints of their existence. Thick, high hedges that bordered fields and thickets clustered by streams surrounded patches of open ground where a fox need only go if hot on the tail of a mouse or being chased by desperate dogs. Foxes lived on as the cunning, secretive creatures in folklore and fairytales, only stopping to take a bow if draped around the shoulders of a lady.

Foxes are striking to look at and their tails are extraordinary. I can't imagine them taking little field mice and the family chooks. But they do, and that's why they're outlawed even in their native countries. Here in Australia, they arrived without ancient ancestors inviting them onto the shore and they will never be welcome. It brings some comfort to read of Russian research into the silver fox. There, scientists are thinking differently about this animal who is despised for no other reason than that the animal continues to be terrified by them, that he can't be tamed.

As a child of the countryside, I was always attached to a pet dog, cat, Sooty the giant black guinea pig and Bobbi the impetuous horse. So it's no surprise that I ended up calling a little russet dog my absolute best friend for almost sixteen years as an adult. With his sleek ochre body, neat triangular face set with two magical black eyes and a full red tail that swept out into a pert white tip, he did look like a fox. We locked eyes through the bars of a cage in a dog shelter just after I'd left the psych ward for another round of re-earthing. I'd decided that life would be less lonely if I had the company of a sentient dog. I'd been given a blue budgie, but it turned out to be unsuitable. The bird took great delight in terrorising me with fly-bys that seemed focused on my eyes, so I soon let the budgie escape outside to continue its descent into hell without my help.

The idea of a dog came not only because of the terrifying budgie, but because my newfound love affair with the guitar put me in a much better space for a carbon-based warm-blooded friendship. However, the calm, regal, little red dog I'd fallen in love with at the pound was immediately exposed as a young tearaway canine backpacker scamming the system to escape. It turned out he had a penchant for freedom, and this passion displayed itself the moment I chauffeured him away from the pound. I drove home with a dog on the steering wheel, on the back luggage rack, on my head, and half out of an inch of open window. When I got him in the front door, he disappeared straight out the back door and wasn't seen again until I found him two kilometres away in a dispute with a rottweiler. It's really hard to call a dog home when he doesn't know his name.

Tigger's territory ended up extending as far as a twenty-foot length of rope allowed. But over time, food, a warm bed and kind words replaced the rope. It seemed he liked the guitar music too, because when I played, he lay there looking at it with half-closed eyes and a smile. Ours became a symbiotic friendship. He: a dog that relied on me for food, shelter and protection. Me: a human scraped out, empty of any affection. Yet I became lovable through his animal eyes—so much so that I could really feel that love. Tigger became my muse for everything.

I know Tigger studied my ways to secure his status in our tiny family. These ways included strange movements entangled in the agony of depression. Sometimes I cried for days without any obvious signs of broken parts. Other times, I hurt parts of my body on purpose and he waited until the sobbing and pain slowed, then timidly came over and rested his weight on my body, his warmth fusing the broken parts back together. He shared my experiences of being chased by UFOs and police helicopters, and the confusion of sleeping outside in cold places when the bed at home would've been warm and safe.

There were intermissions between these intensely painful movements, and we had many great fun times together. I was determined to pay him back tenfold in joy what I took away during the worry times. So many days involved just walking the local country-side and sharing *my* lunch at *his* park. I gave him an

'He put his paw up on my shoulder.'

unlimited supply of love and respect and loads of soft, thick blankets for his bed.

My way of being was tough for Tigger to understand. But he did eventually get it, and he understood me better than any psych support on offer. When the mental health crisis team came out to my house to take me to hospital, he put his paw up on my shoulder, looked straight into my unhappy grey eyes and gave me all the courage I needed. He urged me to go without uttering a sound. He could see the mess we were in with my fading soul, and he knew the team were here to help us both get happy again. At these times, Mum would carefully wrap up his tender little soul and take him away in her car to care for him. I know we all felt gravity multiply as she pulled away.

When I did come home from hospital, oh, what a sweet reunion! I immediately booked little getaways in remote places, staying in tourist cabins, in my tent or blowing my entire pension on a dog-friendly holiday cottage out in the hinterland behind Apollo Bay. We became a happy team again as we travelled via back roads to Tarra Bulga, Cann River and up into the blue-grey dorsal land out the back of Maffra. Me always happy to be driving away from the past, Tigger always

'I immediately booked little getaways in remote places…
blowing my entire pension on a dog-friendly holiday
cottage out in the hinterland behind Apollo Bay.'

happy to be heading into the future. Both of us in for the ride.

These trips were times of joyous reconnection. I cooked majestic egg-and-bacon breakfasts that I shared with him on dewy mornings on sunlit verandahs, then we would spend the rest of the day hiking through rain-soaked forests or along storm-bashed coastlines. Together we climbed precarious rock faces and stalked seabirds, chasing the world-fallen banshees back up into the sky. In the mountains, we meandered through lush forests and along wild streams, over granite boulders, sneaking through slippery moss lands, looking for scary bunyips. In these good times, Tigger always managed to stay a few strides ahead of me, somehow reading my intentions and leading the way.

If our understanding of life is like a dog who sits looking at shelves of books in a library, their words unknowable to him, then love is simple: a happy dog in his favourite park. My dog held no degree. He hadn't read a thousand books dripping in scientific equations of human pathology. He just loved me and I loved him. If I was happy, he was happy. The main ingredient in our successful partnership was this: pure, universal unconditional, unbound, respectful, naive love.

Unfortunately, though, all the love in the world can't stop a war. Tigger was the sweetest bird of peace and the humblest benefactor of provisions, but ravens and vultures were circling higher up.

SOUNDS OF SILENCE

HERE WE GO AGAIN.

Nothing.

∼

I'm lying on the floor of my unit, where I folded up some weeks ago. The blue carpet surrounds me like the giant Pacific Ocean. Desiccated tear-soaked tissues fleck the surface like frozen whitecaps. My island is a pillow, beached on a shoreline of awkward blankets. The TV gurgles noise, no particular channel giving any hint of any particular climate in this godforsaken latitude. Tigger is an island beside me.

I can see the numbers on the wall clock so it must be daytime. A blackened banana sits on the coffee table.

My entire goal in life last week was to eat it. Tick tick tick from the clock. Tock tock tock from my heart. Quiet, alone, nothingness.

With a surge of recalled despair, my body lurches into yet another sobbing fit. I roll over onto my side. My hands grab at the corners of the pillow and I wring them out as if they are filled with water. My eyes scream out in a firestorm of liquefied agony. The pain in my soul is so deep I can't touch it. The primitive aching sounds coming from my throat resemble trees being dragged along the banks of a raging flooded river. There are no words to describe the complete and utter destruction of life within. The sun is dying, and energy has solidified.

Silence fills the space again. It reclaims its throne and I am back in the dark. Night-time rolls back in with faraway birdsong bookending sun-bound life. Out there somewhere in my long-forgotten garden place, an animal stirs. A fox is circling the boundaries of my sleepless dream. His red blood flickers with the asymmetrical rhythm of all desperate and determined creatures.

It's a one-frame cartoon in here. Only the walls evolve, redistributing pigment from daytime pallor to

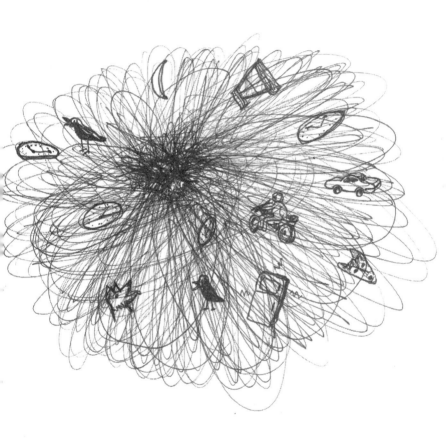

'There are no words to describe the complete
and utter destruction of life within.'

night-time nothing. My bones do the same. My breath grates over a wordless script, waiting for the next bit of story, the next frame to reveal itself. There is none. Just this one long immobile scene revealing nothing I don't already know. The silence in my brain is so vastly different to the deafening roars of psychosis that I crack under the weight of decompression. Beyond my island on the blue floor, there are very subtle clues to existence that give me just enough nourishment to imagine life. They are sounds. A little wall clock plays a rigid click-track, unaware there's no musician tuning up. The ticking clock is the metronome of all life; carelessly waiting for no one. I document all the sounds for the day:

Tick, tick, tick.

Dog barks. Fridge hums. Magpie talks.

Car.

Tick, tick, tick. Wind rattles window. Postman. Doggy door flap. Unidentified click.

Tick, tick, tick.

CONCRETE TUBES AND BEACH HOUSES

Two years since my last psych admission.

There are cameras in the wall plaster. They're filming my every move, capturing all my thoughts and sending the footage back to the control office. I tear off little corners of toilet paper, lick them and then stick them over the tiny holes in the plaster. There's so many of them! I lie down in bed and stare up at the ceiling. There's more up there. I climb up onto my bed and spend ages scouring for holes and sticking down bits of torn paper. Tigger watches me quietly from his mat, letting me redecorate without question.

~

A 'friend' drops in next evening and sits on the third chair from the right, but she places her bag very carefully on her left. That's peculiar. My friend is usually a very trustworthy person, she goes to church and prays a lot. She is teaching me how to hug. (It's been a long road, but I'm getting there.) She never lies, swears or steals. But her demeanour has changed radically since last time we met; her aura betrays her thoughts and warns me to be on guard. She looks up and asks me, 'How are you?' I sense coldness in her tone. Her eyes scan me with a blanketing stare and I realise she's faking it. They've got her and she's on a mission. I'm angry with myself. They're in the room now—how stupid of me to let Them in!

'I'll be back in a minute,' I tell the fake friend in my most casual voice. I walk quietly out the front door, Tigger following. It's 9 pm and dark. Winter has set in and it's cold. I'm wearing jeans and a light shirt. I'm not dressed to go out tonight but I can't go back. This is an emergency; I've got to get away. I quickly walk up to the end of the road, turn left and keep walking. Tigger and I won't stop walking for the next two weeks.

The night passes in jumps and starts, much like my sense of direction. I meander through nearby housing estates and end up in a playground on a hill. The cold air makes my skin burn and there are speckles of rain fritzing about. I see Tigger is shivering too, so I find a concrete pipe and we crawl in to get some rest. But the wind blows through the open-ended tunnel and makes for an inhospitable sleeping place. We crawl out again. My feet aren't as tired as my body, so I keep walking. My mind is stuck on a mantra. It's reminding me, *Keep moving, or they'll find you.* I tell myself that we'll go home as soon as it's light.

Dawn unfolds, but I'm not going home. They'll all be there by now, collecting information. They'll be taking fingerprints off my teacup and swiping DNA data from my cereal bowl. They'll see that I found the cameras in the wall. Even the thought of them becomes evidence. My thoughts have become my enemies. I must not think.

~

The next day, I head into town. I snake through shopping malls, turning left or right at random at each corner. I do my best not to touch anything or, if I do, it's through the cloth of my shirt or using the back of my hand. I don't look at anyone or anything. My eyes give away my identity. Even bricks of buildings threaten me. This town is too dangerous. I need to go into the country.

Night is coming back but I'm not tired. I'm a fugitive and fugitives can't sleep. Hunting eyes are everywhere. Tigger doesn't lead on this long walk. He stays behind me with his nose at my heel. I only take a few moments' rest here and there on park benches during the day. Tigger just coils up with his nose into his tail and takes no real offence at the indignity of another snooze without his mat.

~

That's how it is for a long while. When I'm in the country, my thoughts get stuck and tangled in tree limbs. When I'm in town, the concrete path records my footprints. I'm frightened of murderers lurking in the shadows, but the shadows are my only refuge. Strong wind and saturating rain are the only counsellors of my uncertainty. At night I fold myself up inside squares and triangles of shelter. I can't sleep; my racing ideas and the loud voices of recrimination are too animated to just ignore. I get food for the two of us and coffee for me from sanctified places like church drop-ins and public welfare charities. It all feels faintly normal.

I've always been a wanderer. My childhood unfolded in a rural village clinging to the edge of a moth-eaten back road in the sheep-scattered hills of the Welsh borderlands. My boundaries reached as far as it took to go out and come back before the sun set behind the murky backdrop of the Brecon Beacons. It was the 1970s and the world hadn't yet formed that part of its brain which inhibits unaccompanied children so I dutifully explored fields, farms, churchyards and housing estates without so much as a pixie squeak in my ear. I met and chatted with dairy cows, daisy fields, faceless sheep and faraway trees, contributing to spontaneous podcasts on the weather, mud, flowing water and why my socks had lost their will to stay up and instead were bunched in my shoe.

As a teenager, I found myself wandering a very different land in a very different country. I was bound by concrete and drawn into other people's plans. I became ensnared by the unworldly desires of ghosts; people who found comfort in shedding their skin. Being without solid skin of my own, I copied them. As a ghost, the sunlight stays eternally over the horizon so I explored underground terrariums and discovered landmarks by feel. During my interment, I carved solitary bedrooms out of bus stops, sheds and picnic shelters, and when it was cold I used my shivering as warmth. In summer, I slept on the earth, using my bundled-up hair as a pillow and my arms as a blanket. I was drifting with dead spirits but I was equally free and alive. Had I been a surveyor, I may've just decided to settle and make uncomfortable geography my home, but I get vertigo from stagnated scenery. I have to keep the world moving.

In the distant universe in which I find myself now, the wandering has become haunting. Instead of the scenery moving past my eyes and giving me a sense of stability, it's me moving past the scenery. Everything is a blur. The compass spins without a magnet, incapable of making an informed decision. I've surrendered home for the security of away and it's only Tigger who is giving me bearings. His eyes give the coordinates, his footsteps chart our trajectory and his constant presence provides orientation. I might be losing my mind, but I'm still a good person, so I buy food for Tigger and make sure he always finds clean water to drink. While we both have feet, we will keep moving.

~

After many days of nowhere, we end up at the beach. It's in the middle of night, so the colour and contrasts of daylight have been reduced to grey and black. The weather is horrendous. A gale blows in from no particular direction, carrying a vomit of sea in its mouth. It punches out chunks of the air with furious fists, even attacking itself in its rage. I stare out along the void and see a line of beach boxes much further along the shore. They hint at the distant idea of a summer holiday, so I trudge towards them across the heavy, unfriendly sand.

At this point I really feel Tigger's desire for home. He hangs back. His reluctance drags at me like an anchor. But he follows, trusting me, and we battle on like Mawson, venturing further and deeper into the swirling abyss of icy remoteness. I yearn for a calm, cosy place for Tigger to rest. I can't let him suffer like this.

As we scale the face of the heaving shoreline, the wind grabs my hair and tries to rip it from my scalp, then throws it back into my face with disgust. Sharp bits of sand mixed with sideways rain stonewash my bare skin and stick to my lips. A stampede of angry waves attack the beach. The avalanche of noise is almost too much for my senses, yet it drowns out the pandemonium of my inner turmoil and gives me agonising respite from my own self.

I battle on until I reach the first ramshackle beach box. There's space under the steps that I could fit in, yet it offers no protection from the wind, so I move on to the next one.

This one seems better, but then I have a very vivid mental picture of drug needles and druggie's poo and suddenly the thought of crawling under any beach box seems filthy.

My final chance is a small shed with a broken door. I step inside cautiously, not knowing what to expect. It's dark. The pitching noise outside drops slightly and I feel a moment's relief until I make out two small figures camped on the murky floor. They look up, startled; I apologise and go back out into the wild night. For the first time in weeks, I feel deeply exhausted. My emotions are ragged and they erupt. I wrestle my body back along the tyrannical beach. The rain and the wind take my tears away before they've even left my brain. I'm somewhere around twenty-eight and as old as the dust in my veins.

Tigger is at my heel.

FOX AT THE
BEACH

Fox had kept running. He ran until he was far enough away from the north border of violent beasts to slow the racing blur into segments of lucid information. The smear of taupe and green became bushes and trees, finally breaking down further into grass stems and fallen leaves. He kept the scent of musty creek always on his left, maintaining a sense of home, but the scent of other foxes was very clear and overrode any impulse to dive into a black hole and rest. This was a map he didn't know, drawn by strange foxes. He had to keep moving until his lungs breathed fresh dirt, undefined by suspicion.

Nothing Fox was looking at now was familiar in his map of things. There were cows and fences and trees, yes, but it was as if they'd been picked up, tossed around in the sky and just fallen back to earth wherever they liked. As he moved onwards, Fox recalibrated his map to some logic, but he also knew that his red fur was a moving target among Men and this earth hid their traps behind every unturned stick. He needed to tread more carefully, look extra hard, and decode every tiny molecule of scent and pigment of colour as if they were already arrows.

After many days of unsafe sleep and moons of unrightful crickets, the smell of musty creek becomes salty creek. The dirt under Fox's feet softens and crumbles, making him cringe at the insecure mess between his toes. The thick bushes that thrust spears at anyone trying to reach a hiding fox now collapse meekly with the slightest push. Hardly a breeze floats past without bringing in some kind of unknown smell. The scents remind him of freshly found fur and the taste of undoing that fur and taking it for himself through his mouth.

There's a sound of strong wind growing as Fox continues on. But no tree moves. It perplexes him to hear wind but not see it. How can this be? At last the answer becomes apparent. The wind is a water, a big

'This patch of crumbly dirt is the last bit of
earth before fur runs out altogether.'

water. Maybe a flood. The creek at home sometimes floods, a big brown murky blanket that turns field of cow into creek of cow. This new water-wind is the first time Fox sees the air properly, so he watches it from the 'pushy-bush' for a while, marvelling at it, learning it. The water-wind moves like his mother's fur when they would sit on the bank and watch the late autumn sun setting over the hill, and Fox's mother would tell him a story about another earth where fur was never food.

Fox understands that the earth as he knows it has run out, so this will have to be home. He can smell other foxes here but he knows these are foxes like him. These are foxes who have run out of earth and are not welcome, even by the unwelcomed. This patch of crumbly dirt is the last bit of earth before fur runs out altogether.

THE MEETÎNG

I ARRIVE BACK AT THE car park like an old broken car. Puddles of muddy water form in giant potholes and I want to climb down into one and let the earth soak me up. I can't go home. I can't stay here. I can't go on. I stand useless for a while in the dark, with the rain and wind just flowing through me. Tigger waits for my decision.

It's at times like this I have to accept that life doesn't stop, even if my mind decides it should. It just ticks on. My left foot eventually takes a step forward, then my right, then another left, then another right again. My wobbly legs drag me along a little gravel track weaving up through the dunes. I finally reach a surf lifesaving club built on sandy ground. I see a dimly lit area out the back of the building and my feet become moths. Here

I can finally get away from the weather and pounding surf. Safe at last.

I push my spine down into the corner of the dry space and I huddle my creaking, wet knees up to my numb chin. Tigger curls himself up into a tight fist beside me. It's freezing cold, but dry. The orange glow of the small outside light gives me a sense of warmth. I stare blankly through aching eyes into the inky space of a sand dune covered in prickly bushes. I crave my darling bed. My lovely warm blankets, my soft dry pillow. Now I really wish I was home. My mantra fires back: *Keep moving or They'll find you!* Shut up, you stupid, stupid voice. *No, you're the stupid one, for letting them catch you*, it snaps back. I'm too tired and sad to argue, so I let it win. Again.

At this point, I see a shape shift in the darkness in front of me. I expect it's another black bear or slinky black puma. I've seen so many lately. Tigger doesn't stir so I wait for another shifty shape to mumble across my senses. To my surprise, and in one quick unfussy movement, a powerful red fox is sitting opposite. He looks directly into my face. I can't believe it! A wild red fox is sitting *right in front of me!* Why don't I ever have a camera when I need one? This is *not* a hallucination,

'I push my spine down into the corner of the dry space.'

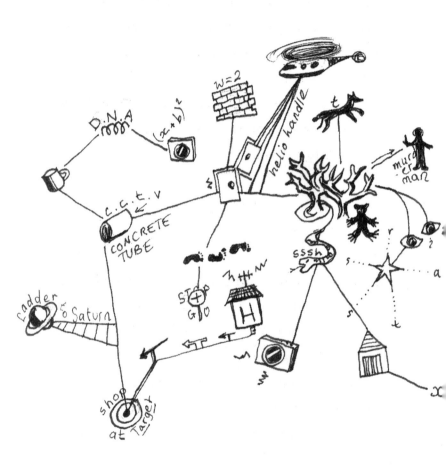

'Keep moving or they'll find you.'

I inform myself defiantly. I tell the fox as well. Even Tigger has noticed him and clambers up into a seated position. He doesn't make a noise or raise a single hackle. He sits and looks, like me, like the fox. We stare at each other.

The orange light and the rain make the fox's red coat glow. A brush-like tail flows out around his side and then curls to rest in front of him. I look at his all-too-close facial features. A tiny, pointy black nose sweeps out into flashes of white fur on each cheek. I look at his two oversized ears, pointing straight up to the night sky. His gemstone eyes are locked on mine; I see they could be made from parts of the universe itself. I get lost in their exhilarating intensity and then realise I've been staring far too long. I worry I've offended him, so I politely look away.

He doesn't flinch. I wonder how much longer this wild animal is going to stay sitting there in front of a pathetic shivery human. I cast numerous sideways glances at him, filling up my memory. But he still doesn't move.

I start to feel very uncomfortable. Do foxes eat people? Especially bedraggled paranoid wanderers,

'A brush-like tail flows out around his side
and then curls to rest in front of him.'

in the middle of night, in the middle of winter, in the middle of nowhere?

I have thoughts of my last moments on earth: a wild fox in my face, biting into my jugular vein and pulling out bits of my throat. The surf lifesavers will only find parts of me next time they meet. Which will be six months from now, in summer. Oh boy, this is going to be long and painful. Then I compare it to my recent life on earth and my even more recent prayer to disappear into a pothole. I come to the frightening conclusion that God is real and he does answer the prayers of the completely desperate. With a dash of Catholic theatricality, of course.

I wait a while, then decide to relax. I let go of my tight grip on my knees. I slowly, slowly stretch out my aching legs in front of me and cross one on top of the other, just to show how casual I am. The fox still doesn't move. I'm beginning to wonder aloud if this fox is in fact a big old classic hallucination, just like the bears and pumas.

As if the fox understands my words, he gently shakes his majestic head and says, *I don't see many humans here at this time of year. Why are you out in the middle of this cold night?*

I'm genuinely surprised. I didn't expect that, but nothing really shocks me anymore. I've become the Queen of Cool around the unexpected, so despite my tattered logic slightly outweighing a talking fox, I play along. 'Because I can't go home. They're after me and I'm not safe anywhere anymore.'

Why are they after you? You seem quite harmless. Did you steal a chicken?

'No, I did not steal a chicken!' I snap. Foxes are predictable after all, I think. 'They're after me because They think I'm unwell. But I'm not unwell, I just have a different way of doing things and They don't want to understand.'

Yes, I actually know that story well. Humans don't like me either. Do you humans hold chickens and rodents as gods?

'Gods? Ha! No. We eat the chickens and little creatures are protected species.' I imagine my answer spreading out through fox communities and fundamentally solving the whole problem. 'Do you know you're in the wrong country for foxes?' I ask, expecting he won't.

Yes. I live every day knowing that I'm on the wrong earth, and I try to tread very carefully. I know my ways don't suit humans at all. But I can't go home either. What is a fox to do?

'You could make friends with humans,' I offer. 'Then you'll sleep on soft earth, with plenty of warmth and food. Humans will look after you instead of chasing you away.'

If I make friends with humans, and I become a common dog, what will happen to the way of the fox? Will it become instead the way of the human?

'I think you'll change the way you do things, but you'll still be known as a fox,' I reply.

So, I will wag my beautiful fox tail instead of using it for warmth and as a symbol of pride; I'll bark and whimper when I see humans, instead of using my many skills in quiet subtlety; my earth will turn against me and become hard concrete instead of gentle grass; and the many seasons of dirt I learned from my mother will become one long dry summer granted me from humans.

Fox looks at me with his deep radiant eyes. His question tugs at my humanness and I am ashamed for suggesting such an idea. An edgy breath of wind catches up with our conversation and makes his coat shimmer like a shoal of tiny fish in clear Atlantic water. He tilts his head gently to one side and flicks the very end of his tail in a way that suggests slight irritation.

'There is your answer.'

Is it really worth it? Fox asks finally, but I'm unsure who the question is directed at.

I consider my answer carefully. 'If you want to live.' It's all I can come up with.

There is your answer.

With that, the fox stands up. He stretches his regal neck, turns back towards his beautiful tail, and vanishes into the deep unknown of the windswept dunes.

I follow the animal with my eyes but the surging night quickly consumes the fading reverie. Tigger has fallen asleep, curled up in a ball beside my leg. I look down at his fur, little tufts catching in the choppy air. I don't know if he's really asleep or pretending, but I imagine he's thinking of his bed, the morning and the two of us heading out to his favourite park.

DEFEAT IS ONE
SMALL VICTORY

THERE'S A RAIN THAT COMES after the rain. It's when
the storm has moved on and the trees begin a free
jazz session of syncopated dripping. The sky clears to
smudges of blues and grey, the air becomes thick with
the memory of a receding downward tide. Flying insects
and crickets dance and jitter with joy to their new
dawn. The ground, already sodden from the downpour,
can't fill its belly any more. Instead, it offers up a watery
drum skin and the second supply of raindrops land
with a *splat splat splittery splat* as they finally return to
the earth from which they were plucked.

My eyes splutter open to the daylight with the energy
of a rusty old tractor. My body has been stuck in an
unsolved Rubik's cube out the back of this surf club

for too long. It's painful to even try to move. My chin is curled down and inwards to my tummy, but my arms and legs have been set hard at awkward intersecting angles. They refuse to budge. My neck has been exposed to the icy wind and aches with a burning chill. It sends pins and needles right down my spine. Before I have the mental strength to ask my arms and legs to shift an inch, I take a long look to survey my latest bedscape.

The early morning light feels innocent in contrast to the drama of the previous darkness. The imposing wall of black prickly sand dunes that delivered Fox now seems smugly ambivalent, wearing familiar beach colours. The saltbush flutters sporadically in the softened wind and I make out small sandy tracks hidden between tussocks of sedge and the tall ridges of heath. Perfect fox tracks. My searching eyes wish for a while that Fox would step out of the scrub and, in true Hollywood style, endow me with a more dramatic parting phrase—like, *I think this is the beginning of a beautiful friendship*—before swishing his noble head and galloping off majestically into the dunes. But nothing.

Time passes. I unfold myself and get myself as vertical as possible. Tigger unpacks himself with care, finds his feet and stretches out. His back arches in a

'Tigger unpacks himself with care,
finds his feet and stretches out.'

beautiful yoga pose, giving each squashed vertebra space to breathe again. His face opens up into a persuasive, generous well-thought-out yawn, then he snaps his teeth together and licks his lips as if he's just eaten one of Fox's chickens for breakfast. He shakes out his frumpy coat and little drops of damp sand flop onto the concrete. He finishes up his rousing routine by making the funny little expelled 'pfft' noise he does every morning to let me know he's awake. He gently wiggles his own little foxy tail as he gives me a sweet tickly kiss on my chin.

Watching Tigger put his bedraggled coat back on, I finally decide that this is no life for us. Fox has made me realise that I need help to stay alive. It's one thing to exist, it's another to live. I tell Tigger that we're going home. He seems to hear my words and I feel a little glint light up his aura. It gives me just enough strength and courage to permit gravity to do its job and draw me back into orbit.

EARTH TO
GROUND
CONTROL

THE ROAD AWAY FROM THE surf club is long and difficult to navigate. Its ultimate destination is the psych
ward, thanks to the circling poachers ready to nab
the tiring animal. Tigger goes to stay with my mum,
as usual in these circumstances, and although I cry
for his company, I know he's safe, getting the TLC
he so deserves while I rebuild my spirit. Mum tells
me he looks for me constantly, which doesn't help at
all, but she also tells me he's loving his roast chicken
dinners, his plump mat in front of the heater and
twice-daily walks in the nearby parklands with Mum's
two big dogs. I want to get myself better to be with
Tigger again.

Re-entry to the psych ward is always traumatic. It resembles a spacecraft's re-entry into the Earth's atmosphere—lots of fire and smoke, lots of communication about me but not including me, always the people watching, waiting, observing and picking up pieces. And just like NASA, the more you do it, the less people are interested. It's a lonely experience going out into space and back home again, and it gets less newsworthy the older I get. Luckily, as a long-time space traveller I have gathered a small dedicated crew of citizen observers keen enough to follow my progress as a human, not a chunk of expensive metal. Earth to ground control is a tentative connection but it helps that I have made some friends in my worldly time playing music with them. They are there on the shore waving tiny flags when I'm plucked out of the Pacific Ocean.

These are real people, not scientists, who visit me in quarantine. They remind me that the routines of the ward are pathetic, nothing more structured than meal breaks for staff, and that I am allowed to be pissed off that there's nothing to do. I imagine this place is what the universe was like before hydrogen atoms started bumping into each other and making things. I see other people in the ward who are still lost in deep space and can't feel gravity, let alone the privilege of boredom. To experience space time, they cut at their skin with all sorts of found objects, just so they can feel the fabric. Others are still shouting 'No!' at their abusers, who still don't listen. Others cry as if the flood is on the inside and Noah never had an ark. I am lucky. I can make my own ark, I feel the weight of material around me, and 'get fucked' is my new favourite phrase.

The language of the psych ward comes back to me through the days that move as slowly and randomly as a clock with a flat battery. I practise phrases of recovery while chewing on antipsychotics and my mouth and body sputters them both out with equal viscosity. The nurses and doctors all ignore me until I do the recovery tricks well enough for them to pat me on the head and say, 'Good girl.' The fire of the crashed spaceship eventually burns out and I walk out of the psych ward, taking my first steps on dry land. The sliding doors of the adult psychiatric unit slip open without fuss. Every other time these doors have been like glass walls, impenetrable without a staff card, requiring three days of planning and an approved sane escort. This time, the staff look away and I'm permitted to escape.

I step out into the boring hospital car park and land back on Earth. I half expect to hear a nurse calling me back and the other half wishes there was. A few benign-looking people are ambling around outside; others are sitting on concrete bollards smoking cigarettes. I know these to be patients on level one of the Release game—two hours leave. A cigarette in the car park is as far as their freedom extends. I scan the number plates of nearby cars.

Some people aren't patients, but on the way to or from visiting patients in other parts of the hospital. They're obvious, because they walk with purpose, exuding an intent to get away from their footsteps as fast as possible. I wonder if they have any idea what I've just been through; whether they even know what a psych ward is. I settle on doubting the suggestion, because unless they've personally experienced the warping of space and time, how could they relate to the theory? I came in to this place with all the energy of a meteor, and I leave a diluted shadow. The feeling is bizarre and belongs nowhere.

The meds interrupt my perception and I let my worries and florid thinking go. I breathe deeply in the late afternoon air; I haven't breathed real, free oxygen

for six weeks. I let my body relax in controlled incre-
ments, because this might still all be a dream. I might
wake up any second with my face buried in that awful
goddamn plastic mattress.

But no, this is real. I'm out.

~

I go home feeling like an old patchwork quilt handed
down from generation to generation, the colours faded
and the stitches frayed. I'm floppy and worn, my heart
pings with a beat that generates just enough energy to
maintain hope. I dig deep. My soul is ragged and I wish
I could pull that quilt up over my head and just sleep
for a decade, but I fight, I sigh. I search for sublime
inspiration in the mundane. Finally, I see Tigger and
reconnect with his beloved fur. His full existence
provides me with a standing start.

At first I'm scared of every thought, every idea, every
internal commentary I have. I constantly assess if it's
a good thought, or a bad thought. Is this helpful? Or
is this not helpful? I might be paranoid, depressed,
psychotic, deluded, disordered in every word, every
letter, but as time passes and the medication clogs my
creativity, I lose the vigilance. I start to think fluid

'Finally, I see Tigger reconnect with his beloved fur.'

random mindless thoughts, and I slowly assimilate back into the ordinary world.

While I walk Tigger around the park each day, I occasionally have flashes of philosophy that open up in my mind's eye like a mathematical thread on Einstein's blackboard. But then I lose grip on the theory quickly and become aware of my feet crushing the grass and breaking the barracks of tiny grass spiders. My momentary Nobel Prize for Philosophy/Physics/Peace is replaced by a mind-map of tiny flowers and thoughtfully placed feet.

To counteract the tedium of normality, I put my well-developed fear of human spaces on hold and go to a songwriting group in Melbourne. It's run by a band called the Bipolar Bears and the name makes me laugh; it's the first time I've heard of anyone making fun of mental illness. I find out it's a creative space for people recovering from psych wards—but unlike the morbid Beatles-admiration club at the local rehab music group, we're actually asked to write our own songs and then sing them. I'm utterly terrified, but I manage to write a song on my guitar called 'Two-Dimensional Fingertips', which I sing nervously to the group:

I can't touch you, through these two-dimensional finger-tips, I wanna reach out and stop me from falling / How I wish I could let you in, tell you all about everything, cos there's always two sides to every story.

People clap and say it's a good song. It startles me and I shrink from the attention. It hurts to be looked at with admiration almost as much as disdain; it's not familiar. I don't know where to put the feeling, so I put it in my shoe, where I can deal with it later.

Whatever I decide, I think I like it, so I'm hooked. It takes two hours to drive to the workshop and almost three to get home, but it's worth drowning in the peak hour traffic exodus for a few moments of liberated heaven and the feeling of being liked for my music, not my ability to mimic ghosts.

Despite the arduous journey, I go every week, with Tigger riding shotgun in our leaky old Camry, and we both enjoy the company of the other songwriters, who also get the whole psych/music thing. Tigger becomes a proud but nonchalant mascot of the group. Some people start wanting to hug me and I freak out. I haven't been touched without an accompanying act of violence for a long, long time. I can't do it. Other people invite me to their houses to watch TV. Just watch TV. I go but I'm always waiting for the catch, where the needle or the perversion, the sordid request or the drunken abuse comes out. It doesn't eventuate, but my apprehension makes it uncomfortable. I don't enjoy the company and they don't enjoy mine. I make a conscious note not to enjoy going into people's houses ever again. The walls are hands.

Apart from wrangling nice people, the songwriting group is a big win. Because of my understanding of classical guitar, my songs have an extra ingredient of musicality that isn't apparent in most other songs. I know about canons, études and how producing simple, expected phrasing can bring out complex brain chemistry in the listener, otherwise known as satisfaction. And from my one experience at a microphone in year eleven, I know I can sing. In this space I'm being given the microphone and the permission to use it. I feel competent, a status I haven't experienced since I wandered the Welsh countryside until the sun went down. I'm capable, wanted and respected for my individuality.

It still strains me to feel social happiness. The pull of anxiety I feel in a room full of humans still unnerves me. It trumps any skerrick of delight. Reading people is always an overwhelming exercise and I prefer not to practise it. I smell people's different scents with multiple layers of timbre gained through biology and environment, I hear the discordant sibilance and taste unfettered pheromones. I shirk away from looking into people's eyes, which frighten me with unspecified power and erratic scribbling. As I go to the workshop each week, I play music but I learn people. I decide there's something about human faces that takes all my energy to process. It's like looking directly into the sun and working out why you can't see afterwards.

I'm also just not happy. My soul is forever aching for the long-lost memory of spontaneous joy and deep-down peace. But I won't give up on the quest to reclaim this basic human right, so I put myself out there again with an outdoor adventure group organised for people with mental shenanigans. I sign up to go surfing for a day at an ocean beach. It's for people with no experience, just madness. The last time I was at a real ocean beach was the day the rehab music group facilitator decided to take us to Rye instead of playing musical chairs. He was a buff young bloke, able to take on a four-foot swell and dynamic rips. Me and Dave were overweight psych patients, pumped full of seroquel, temazepam and flupenthixol. The musician floated; we sank. I was pulled out by my hair and spent the next three days coughing up water and suffering violent migraines.

With this memory hovering in my mind, I allow a team of physical educators to drag me out into a metre of ocean on a giant piece of foam shaped like a surfboard. My first unscripted piece of joy happens unexpectedly, as I sail along on my fat tummy on my first-ever surfboard ride. I'd always secretly wanted to be a surfie chick. So this fine day, here I am lying prone on a foam board as big as a small boat, a little wave rippling along beside me, carrying my bones of lead along like it was the most normal thing in the world. I look across at the fun-loving foam of the breaking wave cheering along next to me and feel a huge tickle in my heart zone. The feeling of floating and flying at once is just too much for my sad soul to take, so I smile. Big and wide, and I even show my teeth.

It's not long before Tigger also learns to surf. A rehab friend gives me a boogie board for my birthday to help me on my quest for surfing nirvana. Due to the lack of divine waves in Port Phillip Bay, the board quickly becomes Tigger's 'boat'. On warm calm summer

'Tigger beside me on his little boat.'

evenings, the two of us clamber into the old Camry and head down to the local beach, where we launch his boat from the clear placid shallows. Tigger climbs on without any indication of fear and happily awaits his chariot ride out to the bay, with his tongue hanging out in that happy doggie way, eyes blinking softly in the brightness and four feet squared for balance. With the ankle leash safely around my wrist, I gently swim us out to deeper water, being careful to always keep the board at 90 degrees to the lazy waves. There are gleeful shouts from children as we drift past their view. 'Mum! Mum! Look! There's a dog on a boogie board!'

Out in the crystalline aqua-blue water with the late afternoon sun sitting casually back on its haunches, little ripples of sparkly salt water tickling my shoulders and Tigger beside me on his little boat, I could almost admit I am in heaven.

ONCE MORE
WITH FEELING

THIS LONG SEASON OF SADNESS and impossibility lasts ten years, well into my thirties. But as with night-time, winter and stars, time happens and the darkness of a tilted axis is displaced by falling light. One morning I awaken to life as if it were a Christmas present from my long-ago time. I slowly unwrap the layers so as not to destroy the fragile magic, discovering each fresh experience as strange and new. Over this uncharted horizon, I appreciate a slow walk on a sunny day more than anything. That clear sky becomes so blue it sings with the weight of a gospel choir; the scent of a Lorraine Lee rose is so sweet and delicious, it reaches into the bedrock of my soul and paints it with perfume. The reassuring weight of my (acquitted) friend's hug is vital, clean water. Tigger's smile is simply beyond words.

Doing repatriation work on my psyche, I remember that I used to love drawing horses. Although the obsession was cured by owning, and losing, a real horse, I hear about a local TAFE course in *illustration*—a new word that rolls and effervescences in my mind like a Fruit Tingle. I enrol. Walking into my first class, my limbs start to freeze into petrified rock, but, as always, Tigger is with me and pulls me into the rip. He just expects all these new people to begin exclaiming over his cuteness and that will, of course, make me happy. The teacher assigns me a proper drawing desk, a big white table that tilts and holds pencils. I'm smitten; anchored to the desk for the next four years. Tigger becomes the TAFE mascot with an official student pass, and I let him wander around the premises at will, knowing that even the security guards are looking out for him. It takes a while, but I finally feel like a steady constellation has formed in the sky above my head.

My meeting with the fox that painfully long winter gave me an insight to the way I see and experience mental illness, and the lowly place in the health system it bestows me. A fox knows what it's like to be outlawed in the normal and abnormal scheme of things. Despite his wild beauty, he's destined to be a lingering side

'Tigger is with me and pulls me into the rip.'

effect of the past. And, just like my psychic distress, he is a symbol of both disease and determination, of a curse and of hope. But unlike the wolf, the lion or the tiger, all noble symbols of pride and honour, it seems the fox is fated to be in the wrong place at the wrong time, for all the wrong reasons. I know that feeling.

When I think about the wildness of schizophrenia and depression, I find myself on a mission to tame them. But it's not just in my own mind where the judgement lies. Society has a responsibility. Schizophrenia in particular has aspects of goodness that are so rarely honoured. If I take out a few painful bits, and think about rearranging the letters to read *capsize hero* (aka survivor), I know there are traits of creativity and sensitivity in there that are less meaningful for people who don't have to battle for peace. Depression leads me to discover things about life I mightn't ever have considered had I not lived in there so deeply.

If we all started viewing mental ill-health as a little red fox, perhaps we could find ways to tame our unease. We could find a proper, loving home for those awkward parts of our psyche that we find threatening, uninvited and wild. Psychoses and episodes of depression are often the sharp end of a long-unspoken struggle, made up of tension and uncommunicated suffering, built up layer by layer until there's very little room left for something else to 'go wrong'. It's no good just repolishing the stainless steel until it gleams; we need to roll up our sleeves, get in there with all the right tools, and start surveying the elements themselves.

Mental illness is the survival story of a meaningful life in a volatile universe. Just like Fox, who has every right to be wild in his beautiful earth that the universe provided through uncounted seasons of trial and error, we humans have a responsibility to make sure we're allowed to hurt, to feel, to break and to heal each other with explicit empathy—not to lock our crookedness away until the pain is rubbed out of its wound.

If we decide to keep the paradox of Fox alive in our souls, we need to make sure he is safe and respected. Souls need to receive real music and art made by wounded storytellers to grow strong, and friends who understand our journey and listen to our stories. My own faith in the Bigger Wheel—a wheel I call God—is an extra bit of oomph in my armoury that I've earned rather than learned. Nothing comes and goes in my life without first being tagged and tested by the master engineer, or whatever trade we decide upon. My soul has a far greater tale to tell than the transient fables of my mind, and our collective stories go back to a time before our sun was a single spark, and will continue until the very last atom winks out.

The fox inside this story could go on and become tame, hanging around the surf club kiosk at 6 pm every night for the daily offcuts and a creeping pat by human hands. He might end up with an Instagram account—'Mornington Surf Club Fox Mascot Goes Surfing'—and gain thousands of likes and followers around the world. I doubt it. More likely, the ranger will poison him to death. His world is finished there at the beach, where the incoming tide devours all sand again, again, again.

If the universal law of entropy is where energy is conserved in seemingly random chaos, the antithesis of this is life. We humans crave order. We seek out and try to subdue anything that defies our passion for structure. We build systems and fences around ill-defined circles and intersecting, crooked lines. We are the antipsychotics of the universe, and this biology is what makes us rare and unique among stars.

As for the fox who escapes, I wonder what will become of his trademark brush tail at full pace across the cow fields, his athletic antics in the big snows of Siberia, his folklore of cunning and quick speed in the forests of England. There, to me a fox is the totem of courage, determination, creativity, resourcefulness and defiant beauty. I want Fox to stay the wise animal of spirit guides and the highest badge of honour for outwitting fate when everything is against you. I'm all for the underdog.

A mind is the Field of Cow in Fox's story. Cow understood their time and space on earth was limited and dutiful. They realised their atoms were bound by a single contract that states what comes, goes and what goes, comes. The field is where life inhales and exhales with the same breath. If we practise our presence well, not an ear will wiggle. Keep looking for your place, keep hoping for your peace and keep expecting a good life, even if today is not. And when you do find your place on the Earth, savour the taste of your win. You deserve to be here as much as anyone.

'Over this uncharted horizon, I appreciate a slow
walk on a sunny day more than anything.'

A LETTER FROM A DOG

Dear Inventor of Foxes and Dogs,

I expect you are nothing less than good. You have great love for us, and that is why I'm so thankful for the posting you have given me. For the most part, it brings me much joy and eagerness to do my job.

However, at this present time, I find myself in a perplexing situation, which leads me to write to you on behalf of myself and a fox I met recently, who is equally concerned (he gave me permission to speak on his behalf). It is in the simple comfort of knowing you will read my words that I find the strength and courage to continue.

The past few months have seen my friend low. I'm not sure what the ailment is, as it is most peculiar—one minute weeping like she's lost a child, the next we are running from a most dreaded assailant (although I have never actually seen him or her in the flesh).

At this present time, we have been walking for many days and sleeping in unfamiliar places. We are searching for something—what, I'm not sure, but we are looking in all sorts of places until we find it. My friend has not eaten and drinks very little, but to her credit, she always makes sure I have a satisfied tummy and protects me with her side when we do sleep.

Of course, I am sure we will find what we are looking for soon enough, and will return home safely to our own beds. But for now, we must continue our journey. I will gladly obey and protect my friend with all my being. I love her so much, and I know she loves me in return; I see her heart is bursting with love.

Thank you again for putting your full faith in dogs and, to a lesser extent, foxes: mere creatures so lovingly made from spicks and specks of dust. I will honour you and make you proud you invented me, and be sure to protect your daughter, my eternal human friend.

Regards,

Tigger

ACKNOWLEDGEMENTS

I pay my respect to Woi-wurrung people of Wurundjeri-willam and Boonwurrung people of Bunerong Country of the Kulin Nations. Thank you for welcoming me on your beautiful country that I wander under the spirit of Bunjil, which I hope to tread lightly and leave as I found.

Thank you to my family – my deepest gratitude and respect especially to my parents who have always provided, protected and persisted without question, because no matter what the weather, the sky is always love.

To my publisher Robert Watkins, the most caring, wise and ethical literary professional I could've possibly hoped for – thank you. Without your brushing away of dirt, Fox, Tigger and me would still be in pages covered with soil. To all my support team barracking for me at Ultimo Press who have each woven golden threads through this much enriched presentation of my story.

My sincerest gratitude to my precious Tigger-y friends who chiselled away at my marble heart with all the love (and tears!) of an artist – two astounding women Virginia Rogers, Helen Morris, and one remarkable Phil Heuzenroeder from Wild at Heart Community Arts. You gently pulled, tugged and untwisted the fibres of my tangled being until I became a much happier human.

To the writers, mentors and disabled literary sector power movers – Fiona Tuomy and Jax Jacki Brown, for being pioneers in access and inclusion and setting Fox up with invaluable support via Write-ability program at Writers Victoria and ultimately awarded me the prize of meeting my brilliant publisher. Thank you with a sky full of fireworks to my writing mentor, Lyndel Caffrey. What an incredible privilege to work under your guidance; you wore the clothes of Fox's story, tested the fabric until every word had a stitch and polished the buttons with me until the story glowed.

Thank you to my brilliant 'schizy' artivist mates who share similar paths beside my story in this book. Mine is not unique by any means. I'd like to especially acknowledge long-time friends who walked with me and Tigger – Steph, Kevin, Ross, and Sandy Jeffs who happens to also be the literary royalty of books who I shadow with humbled footsteps. Thank you, Sandy. My hands go up in celebration to all my Schizy Inc friends, near and far – you're an awesome tribe of cheeky mavericks. Keep doing what you're doing, because you're the ones who don't rock the boat but rock up in a sea-plane and throw out pool noodles!

My thanks also to my quiet supporters who not only set me on some pretty cool railway tracks, you continue to make sure the train doesn't ·fly off into the side of a hill – Fiona Cook, Selene Bateman at Auspicious Arts, and Sonya Pemberton, three extraordinary women with minds I adore sneaking peeks of. Carly Findlay for your guidance and encouragement shared from your hard earned but world-leading advocacy; old Doveton friends (the good sort); Dianne Stephens for your awesomeness when I was pretty ordinary; the saving grace of GROW Psychology; and to Rohan Forster, thank you for serenading me with your beautiful voice and sharing with me the ultimate joy of sunshine, even if the coast looks far away.

Finally and universally, thank you to my bestest friend ever, Tigger. Looking forward to our holiday in the bush . . .

Rest in peace, my friend.
www.heidieverett.com.au